'80

80

1981

STORE

Nettie and Sissie

Nettie and Sissie

The biography of Ethel M. Dell
and her sister Ella

BY

PENELOPE DELL

their adopted niece

HAMISH HAMILTON

LONDON

First published in Great Britain 1977
by Hamish Hamilton Ltd
90 Great Russell Street London WCIB 3PT

Copyright © 1977 by Penelope Dell

SBN 241 89663 0

Printed in Great Britain by
Western Printing Services Ltd, Bristol

To my family past and present

ACKNOWLEDGMENTS

I wo u l d like to thank the following people for kindly searching their memories and their photograph albums and thus giving me much valuable time and help in piecing together this biography of Ethel and Ella, especially those who allowed themselves to be put on to tape: Mrs. L. Adams, Mrs. E. J. Banger, Brigadier E. V. Bowra, Mrs. Patricia Churchill, R. H. F. Dell, Mrs. J. Davies, Mrs. A. H. Dowson, Mrs. M. Evershed, Miss M. Fentimen, Sir John Gielgud, Ms. Victoria Glendinning, Mrs. M. Metcalf, Dame Joan McLaughlin, Mrs. M. G. McDonnell, Alan McKay, Mrs. A. Orange, William S. Parrott, Hayward Parrott, Miss J. Parr, Professor Sir David Smithers, Col. John Savage, Mrs. L. Savage, Mrs. V. A. Sharp, B. A. Sheppard, Mrs. Talbot, Ms. Jean Taylor, Mrs. J. Wright, and the Rev. Marcus Ward.

Without the encouragement of R. E. S. Tanner, J. A. Tanner, D. A. Tanner, and Lena Wickman Rainbird this book would never have been written; to them my most grateful thanks. I am greatly indebted to my editor, Roger Machell, for patient and helpful advice.

To A. P. Watt and Company I extend my warmest thanks for their great generosity in allowing me to quote so extensively from the books of Ethel M. Dell.

The Church Schools Company, the Victoria and Albert Museum, The New York Public Library, The British Library, The Equitable Life Assurance Society, and Barclays Bank have given much useful advice, I am most grateful to them for their willing help in searching records.

The extract from Edward Thompson's *The Other Side of the Medal* is reprinted by kind permission of the author's literary estate and The Hogarth Press; extracts from letters to A. P. Watt & Son and to the Pinker literary agency which are now in the Henry W. and Albert A. Berg Collection are reproduced by permission of the New York Public Library (Astor, Lenox and Tilden Foundations).

P.D.

CONTENTS

ILLUSTRATIONS

Between pages 64 and 65.

PREFACE

IT is not usual for middle class families to be able to trace their ancestors for more than a few generations. Yet Ethel M. Dell could run her fingers up a pedigree which reached back to the middle ages, showing that one of her forebears was William of Wykeham, Bishop of Winchester, Chancellor of the Realm, Founder of New College, Oxford, and of Winchester College.

He was a wealthy statesman, priest, and scholar, and would certainly have approved of his great niece, of nineteen generations later. Though the fourteenth century was rude, crude and direct, it was also bound up in religious practices and beliefs. Nothing that Ethel ever wrote could have offended either the moral or religious thinking of that time.

Yet, in the early part of the twentieth century when Ethel was first being published, nicely brought up young girls were forbidden to read her novels. They had to beg, borrow or steal copies which they then read avidly, while hidden in attic, or airing cupboard. The late Nancy Mitford was one of the many.

That this should have been so, shows that Ethel was a brave innovator and that the so-called 'fast' twenties were still both cautious and prudish. Ethel was a child of late Victorian England, yet her stories abound in explicit and passionate detail. In order that they should be acceptable, she made them highly moral, just as to this day certain publications point accusing fingers to indicate 'Isn't this appalling, shocking behaviour?' and then give us all the intimate details. Ethel charged her writing with this virtuously high tone, yet did not drown the story so effectively that reading her became an exercise in moral hedgehopping.

Though Ethel's eager prose is full of irritating clichés, her books, with their fast-moving episodes, somehow hold the reader's attention. The very fact that they are designed to warn the unwary, and hold up a finger of caution to the innocent, makes them much more exciting to read. It is titillating to be told, so deliciously and explicitly, of the very things which are taboo.

Ethel holds up her finger and shakes it, indicating disapproval but at the same time behind her hand she seems to hide a smile of indulgent complicity. Herein lay her discernment of human frailty. Where other women novelists would indulge in downright moralising in order to get published, Ethel merely shook her head and looked the other way. Once in print, her readers could not have enough of her.

At the time that they were written, Ethel's books seemed shockingly lucid. No woman novelist had ever provided a woman's eye view of the approaching lustful man. She spares her readers no detail of what ensues, yet she is never pornographic, never vulgar, there is no shedding of clothes. Heroines defend their honour when assaulted by villains, but not before being exquisitely tempted, and escape in time for just such another day. Heroes, usually ugly, go through personal fires of hell to save the virtue of their loved ones. Villains, handsome and callous, do dastardly deeds in their efforts to deflower the women for whom they had passing passions.

Ethel's moral tone was irreproachable. Had she written in Latin William of Wykeham might have chided her for grammatical lapses, or lent her a lexicon to widen her vocabulary. But he must surely have agreed with the idealism of the tales she told. More often than not she took biblical quotations as the themes on which her books were composed, and sent her heroes and heroines on their knees in supplication should temptation assail them. When their prayers were answered they were transported with delight and would kneel down and praise 'Him' at their open windows, listening with half an ear to the dawn chorus.

Ethel's heavenly 'pegs' made her acceptable, her passionate content irresistible. She had found a mixture that could be swallowed undiluted, enjoyed, and yet still perform its duty. It was strictly adult reading, though, and not even the moralising whitewashed the purple passages. They were too hot for the tender mind. That these tales were neither stuffy nor pious speaks for her lively talent as a story-teller.

Throughout the Dell pedigree, the name Parrott can be traced from the earliest times, together with Fiennes (Saye of Sele), Danvers and Gardener, three of these last being LL.D.s and Fellows of New College, Oxford. Dells are present as far back as the 1690s, two also being Fellows of New College in 1776. Three times Dells and Parrotts intermarried; though the Parrotts have continued to proliferate, this particular Dell line has now come to an end.

Ethel never mentioned her ancestors; with her unassuming personality she despised the social climber, fought for the unpopular, and, at a distance, admired the well-born, provided that they ran true to her ideals.

Ethel's lineage would have interested her only as useful background for her stories. No one could have cared less if her blood was blue or green, in contrast to her sister and brother, whom she gently teased for being class-conscious. She had, nevertheless, romantic and passionate instincts, high ideals and a tensely rapturous nature. All these were wholesomely fused with a good and remarkably innocent mind. Fortunately she had a sense of fun, without it she would have been unbearable.

ONE

Childhood

ETHEL MARY DELL was born on 2nd August, 1881, at 61 Hayter Road, Brixton, Lambeth, then a fashionable suburb of London. The second daughter and youngest of Vincent Dell's three children, Ethel arrived unexpectedly early. Irene Elizabeth, or Ella, the elder daughter, though still only three and a half years old, had already performed her only public act, namely presenting a purse of money to Princess Alexandra. On Ethel's arrival, Ella was to experience her first pangs of jealous possessiveness, a fault in her character that was to spoil much of her adult life. Reginald, or little Reggie, born between the two girls, was never of much account, a weak child whose not very strong personality was already in process of being swamped by Ella.

Irene Dell, née Parrott, did not have an easy time giving birth to Ethel, who was not only premature, but took her time. The midwife who had been sent for in such haste (Ella thought she remembered the maid rushing down the path, her cap tails flying in the wind) stayed several days before Ethel decided the moment was appropriate . . . a long haired, vocal baby with exquisite hands. Irene had a haemorrhage and to Vincent's extreme annoyance the midwife counselled him to stay at home, for at least that day.

To break routine and miss going to the City was an irritating trial for a man with Vincent's strong sense of discipline. He had been with the Old Equitable Insurance Company since he was seventeen, without a single day lost from the office, except for official holidays.

Since his father had suddenly died at the early age of forty-nine, he had been the sole wage earner for his mother and her family of six younger children. He was working his way up to be chief clerk, a position of great trust and responsibility and the post which his father had held until his death.

1

Vincent at twenty-eight was already there, where he was to remain for the rest of his working days. Ethel's birth was engraved on his memory as a wasted work day.

She had arrived into a close-knit family, with Ella well established, even at three and a half, as the image of her father both in temperament and looks, and Reggie, the baby, already under Ella's influence. Protestant mother Irene, serene in the knowledge that she had done her duty in producing a son and already considering herself a cut above the Roman Catholic Dells, had tried to alienate Vincent from the rest of his brothers and sisters. Not very successfully though, as the Dells all lived within walking distance of each other, until they either married or entered the church. The exception to the pattern was the odd household of Aunt May, whose bachelor brother William lived with her, hoping against hope that his loved one would one day be free to marry him—a happy event which never transpired.

To fill up their otherwise empty lives Uncle William and Aunt May were constantly at the beck and call of their nephews and nieces. Aunt May was hideous, or as Ethel would have written more kindly 'not beautiful'. Uncle Will was gay, dapper, and rather good looking, with a penchant for spats and soft cream chamois gloves. He collected watercolours. Both useful and irritating, they were, as a couple, a refuge in times of trouble.

At one point Aunt May's sister, Marie Louise, home on leave with her four sons from India, found herself at her wits' end to know what to do when her last born child, a girl, suddenly developed scarlet fever. The doctor said the rest of the family must get out of the house at once. Aunt May came to the rescue, took her brother-in-law and his four sons into her home and fed them so well that the entire family burst out of their clothes. When the girl, now Dame Joan McLaughlin of Stanbrook Abbey, asked them how they had enjoyed it, they happily pointed to their waistcoat buttons which would no longer meet.

Ethel flew into this organised pattern of behaviour like a strange bee from another hive. She was buzzed around, and found to be rather fragile but not aggressive so was fed delicacies and cosseted by all.

Ella championed her childhood, concentrating all her attention on guiding little 'Nettie' out of trouble. If Reggie, out of jealousy, tried to tease Ethel, Ella rushed to her assistance, roughly pushing Reggie away. Ella became big, tall and awkward, Reggie stayed weedy, and Ethel grew elegant and very gentle

Irene loved her last-born with a tenderness that she had never been able to feel for the other two. She seemed to be nearer Ethel in spirit. Both were quick-witted, observant, and full of imagination. Later in life, both found other people of absorbing interest; they would endlessly discuss mutual friends, trying to find out why they were or were not happy, or behaved as they did. When still quite young, Ethel showed identification with the under-privileged, and her sympathy for others remained a strong characteristic all her life.

Brixton was hardly smart, yet Hayter Road, situated about fifteen minutes from Clapham Common, could have been called a good middle-class district. Vincent had been born nearby in Cavendish Terrace, Clapham Common. Always wayward, Vincent had slipped from the narrow confines of the Catholic faith, and was therefore the religious black sheep of the family. His marriage to Irene Parrott, daughter of a well-to-do Midlands solicitor whose family were strictly Protestant, underlined his breakaway. Irene had cut Vincent and their family off from the mainstream of Dell 'Massing'. His children were to be called 'little heretics, poor lambs', by their Dell relatives.

Ella recalled her mother telling her to have nothing to do with priests, as they would 'get hold of her'. A fear of priests, and their flowing robes and birettas, haunted both girls all their lives.

Yet later in life Catholicism had a great fascination for Ethel. She was to conceive saintly men and women for her main characters; much of her writing could have been called hagiographic, were it not for its sentimental tone.

Ethel was a good dreamy little girl who inspired a type of protective behaviour from Ella, which became possessive; Ethel was Ella's property, her pet, and this led to complications later on. It is, however, abundantly obvious that Ethel would never have continued her struggle to be a writer had it not been for Ella's championship and faith in her. Ethel herself was the first person to acknowledge this.

Ethel early showed signs of creative imagination. Her dolls

became real people whose doings she endlessly discussed. Ella, always good with her hands, made clothes to fit the stories, once being begged to make chamois leather gloves for a boy doll, so that he could go to London, just like Uncle William Dell, properly dressed and 'looking dandy'. On another occasion she was given a sailor doll which had to be transformed into a country gentleman, just like Uncle William Parrott. This was more difficult as it entailed using tweed, and making a cape and deerstalker hat. Ella surmounted the problem by tricking the maid into leaving the flat iron a little too long on a pair of her father's trousers, which thus became unusable and available to be cut up for dolls' clothes.

Grandpa Parrott had been a well-to-do and highly respected solicitor, his practice was at Stoney Stratford, in a firm originally founded in 1775. The town straddled Watling Street between Northampton and Towcester. Granny Parrott, also an Irene, was a large-boned, heavy-jawed, and much loved woman who had a charismatic personality which obliterated any physical defects. Ella, Ethel and Reggie all adored her. To go and stay with Granny Parrott was the most delightful experience of their childhood. Ella felt a particularly strong bond with her Granny, and was eventually left her collection of Buckingham lace, and books handed down to her from her grandmother's grandmother, Elizabeth Osborn, who had married Michael Smith in 1750 at Northampton. A pair of pencil and wash silhouettes of Elizabeth and Michael also came her way.

This unusual interest in the past was later reflected in Ethel's work; here was real proof of exactly what her forebears read, wore, and looked like, and in her many stories about India, not only were her descriptions of places reasonably correct, but she could seldom be faulted on dress or customs whether civil, military, Indian or Anglo-Indian. Ethel never visited India, in fact she only once put foot outside England, to pay a much regretted visit to the South of France, which she incorporated in her book *The Serpent in the Garden*.

Not only was Granny Parrott a collector of Buckingham lace, she made the best perry in the district from pears in her garden, pear trees that still stand there. Her seed cake was faultless, made to be eaten while drinking Madeira wine, between 'kindly' visits in the chilly winter mornings. These visits to people in need took place almost daily. She would pack a basketful of simple food that she considered would be useful, cakes, pies, a bottle of wine, or warm clothes for the needy. As they grew big enough, Ella and Ethel took it in turn to help her carry her basket. In the year 1881 John Parrott, their grandfather, had started a Charity for Poor Ladies; that it was the year of Ethel's birth was a coincidence rather than deliberate, but it lent an added zest to the girls' efforts to help their widowed granny on her rounds.

Stoney Stratford had been the centre for making Buckingham lace since the sixteenth century when Huguenot refugees settled in the area. When the Dell children stayed there, there was still a school for lacemakers at No. 149 the High Street. The Parrott home, Tower House, was at No. 96 the High Street, only a few steps away across the road. It combined an office on the ground floor front, with a separate front door leading to the upper floors. The back of the house gave on to a large garden. This garden was the delight of the Dells, little Londoners that they were. Here they first heard the songs of blackbirds and thrushes, so often brought into Ethel's books, and were allowed to climb the apple and pear trees and bark their shins, when sympathy, rather than a scolding, would be given.

There was also a beloved King Charles spaniel, a spoilt and unforgettably smelly dog who welcomed any amount of cuddling from Ethel. She often seemed to be on better terms with animals than people.

Over the garden wall could be seen the tower of the ruined church of St. Mary Magdalen, gargoyles at each corner grimacing down at them as they played hide and seek among the lilac bushes, or brushed up their expertise with Diabolo, the latest craze for children.

On the street side of the house which is built of red brick in Queen Anne style, a bow window overhangs the black office front door. This gazebo, constructed of wood and painted white, catches the eye at once, and featured in the lives of the Parrotts from the time they bought the house in 1775. It was an excellent place for spying on passers-by in the street. That bow window, so discreetly curtained, usually screened a pair of alert eyes. In the racing season and particularly at Easter, it was fun to watch the carriages full of gaily dressed racegoers, passing by in the mornings, full of hope, smiles and pretty clothes, on their way to Towcester, and returning rather the worse for wear in the evening.

Granny's son, Uncle William Rose Parrott, lived next door, with his wife and two children, born a little while after the Dells' children. William and Evelyn came in to play with their cousins but were far more in awe of their Granny than Ella or Ethel were. William remembers how shocked he was at Ella's familiar, offhand manner. After Church on Sundays when the whole clan had sat in the Parrott pew and listened with boredom to the sermon, there was a gathering in Granny's drawing room, to drink special golden sherry. All the children were allowed to have a glass, and if they were very small were permitted to water it down.

At this time, 1893–5, sewage was collected once a week on Monday nights in the High Street. Squinney Radcliffe, the driver, came round with his tumbril and horse, starting his rounds at eleven at night. All windows were firmly shut while his men went to the back of the houses to collect and return the sanitary buckets. All water was drawn up by hand pump, and baths were taken once a month in a round tub in the bedroom. The streets were paved with cobbles or 'pibboles'; all transport was horse-drawn except for the occasional pennyfarthing bicycle. Granny wore a little black lace widow's cap with tails which hung down over her ears.

Ethel was only five when John Parrott died leaving Granny mistress of the larger house; her son William Rose, next door in the 'Colony', kept a kindly eye on her financial position, which must have been very comfortable. William's father had built up an excellent clientele, and having been a partner, he simply took over.

Opposite the house stood the Cross Keys inn, where carriage horses were unhitched to be walked round the yard before being rubbed down with handfuls of straw, their owners meanwhile revitalising themselves inside. This operation could be watched from the bow window, but it was much more interesting to be closer. Ella used to take Ethel and Reggie firmly by the hand, and stand on the cobbles just inside the yard to watch the ostlers busy about their tasks, Reggie fidgeting as he was afraid of horses, and Ella keeping an eye on the gazebo window, in case they were summoned home. Ethel adored all animals and would fearlessly stroke the horses if she could get near enough. Looking across the road to Tower House from this courtyard, the Parrott stables could be seen on the left of the house, big enough to house a carriage and pair. They are there to this day even to the hay racks and the cobbled yard, the big wooden doors still hang well, though seldom opened now.

That the house and stables were built over an old churchyard, belonging to the Mary Magdalen tower next door, might account for the many times that Ethel reported seeing 'things in the dark' and hearing 'funny voices' which did not in the least alarm her, but sent Reggie into tears, and brought scorn and disbelief from Ella.

TWO

Young Girls

THESE EARLY visits to Granny Parrott were made with their mother. A horse and cab would be hired which took them across London to Marylebone Station, where they caught a train to Wolverton that slowly puffed across the countryside with a steamy chunter. Both girls would be wide-eyed with excitement, pointing to the unfamiliar sight of a herd of cows, a horse and plough, boats on the river, fishermen, children waving to be waved back at, or horses in a field racing the train. The sudden covering of their ears at the frightening noisy blackness of a smelly tunnel.

Waiting at Wolverton would be the Parrott carriage and pair, the coachman would tuck them in with rugs, and on fine days the hood would be down, Ella and Ethel sitting hand in hand, back to the horses, Reggie and his mother primly facing the way they were going. Stony Stratford was only a few miles away.

Ethel loved the sensuous feeling of being carried along. Later she described a car as 'A Chariot of the Gods, rushing through the air.'

Vincent did not come on these visits, and it is a tribute to Aunt May that he could be safely left behind to be heartily fed every evening.

Later, when the children were in their early teens, Stratford visits were undertaken alone. The cab from Brixton would first take them to the offices of the Old Equitable, near the Mansion House. Here Vincent would meet them, take them round the office to be introduced to Mr. Frampton May, the head clerk, the girls dropping curtsies, then out to lunch in the City before being put in the cab for Marylebone. Ella would be in charge of tickets; very grown-up and responsible, she would engage a porter to put their luggage in the right train. Vincent also taught her to tip. She became the most adept tipper imaginable; with a fistful of coppers she would proffer her hand knuckles upwards, then drop the contents into the outstretched hand with a sharp opening movement, giving a curt nod and smile before turning on her heel.

Ethel never learnt the art, she was too shy and too anxious not to offend, preferring someone else to do it for her. The adult Ethel overtipped but Ella never.

That Granny was known for her cooking and medicinal mixtures was partly due to her own talent and partly to inheriting a cookery book started by her Aunt Jane Smith, her father's sister. Josiah Michael Smith, granny's father had been a wine and spirit merchant in Stoney Stratford, which might account for the liberal use of alcohol in her recipes. Aunt Jane and her sister Martha who never married but lived to a ripe age, were cherished by the Parrotts, a couple of loving and loved spinsters who allowed themselves to be made use of, much as Aunt May and Uncle Will did later on with the Dell family.

Aunt Jane started her book in 1841, when she was thirty years old, and wrote out some hundred or so recipes which cover not only cooking but household and domestic remedies, all written with an exquisite hand, and carefully indexed at the back of the black leather note book. Although the family were in the wine trade, they were not above making their own home-made elder and cowslip wine, nor inventing ersatz preserved ginger using lettuce stalks.

This book puts medical cures for ague, toothache, cramp, rheumatism, and pains in the stomach, between raspberry jam, poison for crickets, whipped syllabub, Harness dye, Iceland moss jelly, and Strengthening Mixtures. These last were definitely kill-or-cure, it is a wonder that Ethel survived to tell her tales as she was a delicate looking child, pale with dark rings under her eyes. No granny could have resisted the temptation to put some colour into her cheeks, by giving her a glass of the following.

Strengthening Mixture.
½ lb. Sarsparilla root, 1 oz. Bark of Sassafras root, 1 oz. shavings of Lignum wood, 1 oz. licorice root.

Method.

The above quantity divided into eight parcels and each should be boiled in a digester kept for the purpose, in a quart of water till reduced to a third. Strain through an earthenware sieve. A wine glass of the mixture two or three times a day. If *White*, vitriolic acid 15 to 20 drops added, and the mouth should be washed with chalk and water after taking.

All three children remembered pinching their cheeks before breakfast, in case Granny should notice a certain paleness and bustle off to her medicine store, triumphantly returning with perhaps the following restorative which might have been lickorish to an adult palate, but must have made the room reel for a child.

Restorative (courtesy of Mrs. Neville),

6 eggs with the shells, the juice of 6 lemons. Beat the eggs, crush the shells rather small, mix all in a basin, and let it stand for three days, stirring occasionally. Boil ½ lb. loaf sugar in ½ pint of water, strain eggs and lemon juice, add sugar and water, luke warm. When cold put in a pint of best Brandy. (or Rum). Bottle and cork tightly. Shake well before pouring out. A wineglassful an hour before rising to be taken.

That Ella in old age had a weakness for both brandy and bromide, may well have been cultivated in her youth by being forced to eat Granny's cooking and drink her potations. A recipe for claret jelly leaves one wondering if people had better heads for wine in those days, what child nowadays could enjoy this special treat, and ask for more?

Claret Jully.

A bottle of Claret. The rind of a lemon and the juice, a small pot of red currant jelly. ½ lb. of loaf sugar, rather more than ½ cup of gelatine and a wineglass of brandy. Boil all together for five minutes, strain, and put into a mould. Serve with cream sauce.

Ethel loved it and several times remarked to Ella that it was a pity that Granny had never given them the recipe. In fact she had, but Ella had not bothered to go through the little bundle of books her mother kept beside her bed, and which were put into a trunk on her death, not to come to light for another fifty years.

Medical recipes would have stemmed from Anne Smith (*née*

Worley), granny's mother, and a daughter of Surgeon John Worley, who, with his brother, Thomas, was listed in 1810 as being trustees of the Stoney Stratford Free School, a Rose and Crown charity which taught eighty scholars who paid only a shilling entrance fee. Later in 1830 amongst the bills which Dr. J. Worley rendered to the Overseer of the town, were the following; bleeding man at the lodging house 1/–. Mixture Irish woman at Cage 2/6 (the Cage being the name for the local lock-up). Amputating the toes of a child, 5/–, powders to Irishman at the Cage. This last man would probably have been one of the Irish navvies brought over to help build the London to Birmingham railway.

The deeds of another brother Edward Worley, although hushed up at the time, caught the imagination of young Ethel. She persuaded her Granny to tell her about this handsome and daring soldier of fortune, who had been Granny's uncle. Ella also listened entranced as his story unfolded and begged for concrete evidence. This was produced, and took the form of a very fine large miniature of Edward, together with a treasure taken from his dead body consisting of an Indian miniature of Rangeet Singh, Ruler of the Punjab, set as a brooch in pure soft gold, behind a crystal 'glass'. Separately there came a diamond ring, which in the opinion of Rangeet was worth the life of the Englishman who had given it in his service.

Here is the reason for both the shame and the pride, and the story of an honourable discharge of duty in the face of distasteful obligation. Edward Worley, having fought in the battle of Waterloo, probably as a Cornet, found himself on the Continent, and rather than turn back decided to search for more profitable excitement. His portrait shows him in Hungarian Officer's uniform, pink cheeked and handsome, having added a 'de' before his surname. This change of scene was not enough for him however, as he is next heard of in the pay of Rangeet Singh, as a soldier of fortune, teaching Pathans how to use muskets, drill in European style, and use the strategy he had learnt from both British training and his experience on the Continent. He was by no means the only European soldier on the staff of Rangeet's vast army, which not only defended the ruler's own territory but frequently raided neighbouring states, sacking towns and bringing back looted gold and jewels.

Had this been Rangeet's only preoccupation, the story would have been vastly different, but in 1832, he came into conflict with the British who were moving north towards his border. There ensued the Battle of Mudkee, the first Anglo-Indian foray before the Indian Mutiny. Edward (de) Worley was in the 'wrong' army, and it is to his credit that he fought to lose his life at once. The disgrace had he been captured would have been unimaginable.

Ethel's imagination must have been stimulated as she listened to this true story about a member of her family. Honour before dishonour, duty first, even unto death, were the keystones of many of her novels, and the inspiration for such idealism may well have been seeded by Edward de Worley.

THREE

Adolescents

IRENE PARROTT had been remarkably well educated for a mid-Victorian girl. She and her brother William Rose may have shared a tutor. The fact that she felt perfectly capable of teaching her three children herself and imparting to them all the knowledge that she possessed, may explain why the two girls, Ethel and Ella, bright and diligent as they were, remained so extremely restricted in their knowledge of the world around them.

Irene taught them from the books that she herself had learnt from, Latin, Greek, mathematics and history, both human and natural, all at least thirty or forty years out of date, and some going back to the early eighteen hundreds. Fortunately in the year 1890, they moved to Ferndale, Polworth Road, Streatham. Ethel was just nine. It was a larger house, close to the common, and here they began to meet children of similar background. Evidently Vincent had reached his peak at the office, and money was not scarce, but another three or four years were still to go before they had any proper schooling. During that time Ella caught scarlet fever; she had a severe infection, all her hair fell out, and the already lanky child grew at a tremendous rate. By the time she was well enough to get up and be with her family, she towered over them all, even her father. As she was only thirteen, it compounded her already awkward and offhand manner and to cover her embarrassment she became haughty and withdrawn.

One of the interesting school books used over the two or three generations of Parrotts is a small black leather volume called Hort's Pantheon. It is an introduction to mythology, with questions and answers. From the pencilled dates it seems that the method was to learn long passages by heart, and recite them aloud. It contained part of Pope's translation of the *Iliad*, and

13

Pitt's *Virgil*; it also covered Indian, Mexican, Egyptian, Persian, Scandinavian, Arabian, and Babylonian myths. There is a wonderful passage that excuses the need for such knowledge in the young. 'In poetry and works of elegant literature allusions are so frequently made to the Mythology of the Ancients, as to render it desirable that young persons should acquire some knowledge of that subject, yet few of the sources whence information of this kind can be derived are sufficiently pure to meet the eye of innocence.

'Before the glorious splendour of truth beamed forth from the Gospel of Christ, upon a darkened world, the pollutions of licentiousness were intermingled with religious rites and compositions. Passions so degrading, actions so shameful, were attributed by the Heathens to the false divinities whom their deluded imagination had devised that from the contemplation of such a spectacle, the delicate mind must turn away with disgust, so that, without some modification, such histories are utterly improper to be presented to the attention of youth. The following introduction to Mythology is intended to obviate this.'

Every chapter begins with a question such as 'Who was Vesta?', in this case; 'Vesta was the daughter of Saturn the goddess of fire, emblematical of the pure vital heat which, being suffused throughout the frame of man, enlivens and cherishes him.' Then to make sure that the tender reader is not quite carried away by these 'myths', the next question asks 'What is the continuation of this fiction?'.

What better grounding could an imaginative child like Ethel need to spark off her own talents? Some of her passages are couched in almost similar vein, needing only the framework of a story on which to hang the passionate flag-waving phrases. Ethel's memory was very good and she could remember exact remarks and their intonation, spoken to her in childhood. Strictly in the bosom of her family she was a very funny mimic, but never outside the close confines of her own house.

It was decided to send Reggie to Dulwich College, for which there was an entrance exam. To make sure of his acceptance, he was sent to a crammer in the City, travelling with his father every day.

Once he had embarked on a proper education, showing a talent for mathematics which neither of them shared, the girls did not see very much of Reggie. He had at last begun to move away from the petticoat environment and taken a masculine interest in life. Ethel missed him, but Ella did not, since she now had Ethel entirely to herself.

Ethel began to write stories about knights in armour. She devoured the Arthurian legends, and read every book on the subject that she could find, while Ella began piano lessons, quickly showing talent. Irene realised that there was little more that she could teach them.

By 1893, when they had been in Polworth Road for nearly three years, Ella being fourteen and Ethel twelve, it was decided to send them both to Streatham College for Girls, five minutes' walk away. Perhaps Vincent had moved to Streatham with this in mind; the College had been established only a year before their move to the district, and he had by now had time to see what the tone of the place was like. Occupying a lovely Georgian house called the Shrubbery, it was run by the Church Schools Company, on the highest moral and educational principles. Its intellectual tone was enhanced by the history of the building, which echoed with the ghostly voices of Fanny Burney and Dr. Johnson. Mrs. Thrale and Mrs. Piozzi used to visit it when it was the rectory of the Rev. James Tattersall. The garden was crammed with temples and summer houses, the grounds running down to Tooting Bec Common. The house itself was remarkably beautiful, both inside and out, containing a fine 'well' staircase, topped by a cupola, an Adam room, a Masonic Temple room, and a priest's hole. All this was entered via a magnificent twin flight of curved steps, leading to a grandiose porch.

The Shrubbery was by far the finest of the Streatham big houses, and there Ella and Ethel repaired every day for the rest of their schooling. Ella took full advantage of the school's interest in singing which was taught by a master who, to the frustration of the girls with good voices, brought his wife to take the solo parts for concerts.

Ethel neither musical nor artistic, concentrated on history, scripture and modern languages, which were taught by the headmistress herself, Miss Van Oordt, a formidably spartan intellectual who thought little of the visual and acoustic arts, and led her best pupils away from such transient joys. Both girls did well, their old fashioned classical education with Irene proving a firm foundation for new knowledge.

Vincent had for some time been suffering from gout, which in those days doctors attributed to over-indulgence in alcohol. Whatever the cause, Vincent, never a man of equable temper, became irascible. Irene withdrew her affection which had never been very warm (he may have frightened her), but Ella managed him well, with a mixture of firmness and humour, while Ethel always remained in favour.

At the Shrubbery (or Snobbery, as parents of children who could not afford the fees called it), there were no music lessons other than singing, so Ella travelled to the Guildhall School of Music in London every Saturday for the last year or so that she was at school, gaining her certificates with monotonous regularity.

Ethel began to write stories for her classmates which were first giggled over and then generally confiscated by the staff. Neither girl had any idea how other people lived, since their parents objected to their bringing school friends home, or visiting families outside the Dell–Parrott range. Reggie, now a scholar at Dulwich, lacked the physical energy to do more than swot at his homework, eat, and sleep. He, too, was banned from inviting school friends home.

The nearest that either Dell girl came to the normal search for sexual knowledge was hearing from other girls at the school about their elder brothers' and sisters' love affairs. Ethel lapped this up, even at second or third hand it sounded deliciously romantic. Ella was much less interested; she was so tall and self-conscious she could not visualise herself ever becoming either physically or emotionally entangled with a man. So she concentrated on music and entertained vague ideas that it might be fun to teach. In 1898 Ella, now seventeen, left the 'Snobbery' and spent two years at the London Royal Academy of Music where she worked hard and obtained her Licentiate. Her voice was a rich contralto; Vincent was more than unjust about it, constantly referring to 'Ella's catawauling'.

Ethel spent much of her last two years at school writing stories for her friends. Vincent was allowed to read them, and took a fancy to his daughter's efforts. He had them privately printed. The first time a budding writer sees himself in print is shockingly exhilarating. Ethel felt both stimulated and encouraged; it does not seem to have occurred to her that there might be room for improvement in the quality of her writing. She began to pour out a stream of stories, and Ella laboriously and lovingly typed them out for her.

By 1898 both girls had left school and Reggie had started being a clerk in London. Vincent was by now suffering increasingly from gout. It was decided to move to the country. They found a larger house at Knockholt in Kent, from which one could travel to London daily by train. So the girls and Irene finally shook the dust of London from their clothes and settled down to be country ladies. Vincent's health improved slightly, and he assumed a jolly country gentleman's attitude at weekends.

Vincent was earning around £600 a year. He could afford a carriage and pair, and employed domestics and a gardener. The Dells began to be called on by the local gentry, and at last it seemed as if the two isolated girls might be enticed into society. No one had realised that the improvement in Vincent's health was only transitory. He began to suffer from high blood pressure and fits of uncontrollable temper. Irene, always neat and prim, withdrew even further from him, while Ethel put it all down in writing to be used later.

On 18th May 1900, the whole family rushed to London to watch the celebrations for the relief of Mafeking from the Mansion House balcony. As they looked, from this vantage point, at the mad milling crowds waving flags, shouting and singing, Vincent pointed at a slim figure of a man trying to wave a twenty-foot Union Jack above his head. 'The young fool' he growled, then peering hard exclaimed, 'By thunder, it's Reggie, just like him, the idiot!' Though Vincent had little affection for his only son, Reggie had on this occasion almost succeeded in making his father proud of him.

FOUR

Young Women

ONCE ESTABLISHED at Knockholt, Vincent decided that he had better do something about his 'girls'. Tennis was becoming a fashionable pastime and was a pleasant way to do a little entertaining and get to know one's neighbours less formally than round the dining-table. Over the old croquet lawn he had a tennis court marked out, and ordered posts, nets, racquets and balls from the newly established Civil Service Stores where he had opened one of the original accounts. He took his girls into town to be properly kitted out with extra full, long white skirts, blouses of Indian cotton with mutton chop sleeves, and straw boater hats. White laced-up tennis boots completed the outfit.

Invitations for the first party went to Sir Waldron Smithers and his wife, who lived nearly opposite, to the Hammonds at the Grange and to the vicar and his wife. For weeks beforehand, Reggie and the girls spent hot evenings practising, a book of rules having arrived with the tennis racquets. The girls served underarm and tripped on their skirts, Ella sent everything out of court, Reggie was constantly looking for lost balls, and Ethel tried to teach her dog to help him.

The great day arrived, the players paired off and Irene, after supervising the preparation of cucumber sandwiches, sat enthroned on a white wicker chair. The games were most orderly, the right calls were given, a missed ball was greeted with 'bad luck', and a less than lopped serve as 'jolly good shot'. It was all painfully polite but somehow, Vincent sensed, there seemed to be no enthusiasm.

At the end of the first set the gently perspiring players were welcomed back to the side lines and congratulated on their prowess; from the dining room window came the trolley of cucumber sandwiches, pushed by a maid, and behind her another maid carrying a large tray covered in tinkling glasses. Irene

18

turned in surprise. She had set out not glasses, but tea cups! Then she noticed Vincent had his arms full of bottles, and was walking extremely cautiously so as not to shake them. 'Well, here we are,' he beamed at the faces turned towards him. 'I thought port would go better than tea with tennis.' He knelt down reverently and uncorked the bottles. The glasses were large, the sandwiches small, none of the players remembered much more about the afternoon except that it was a smashing party. The Dell port tennis party became part of Knockholt history.

What with the Mafeking celebrations, and the midsummer tennis party, October found Vincent's gout and high blood pressure distinctly worse. His doctor recommended him to take three months' leave of absence from the office. The Old Equitable lived up to its reputation and gave him immediate release from duty at full pay. To have Vincent hanging about the house, irritable and bored, did not make for happiness. Ethel shut herself up in her room, and concentrated on writing a series of unreal but idealistic love stories, which Ella read, suggested revisions, and finally typed. Longing for a little independence, Ethel sent them to a number of magazine editors. Ella began to teach the piano, and to sing solos in the church choir. On most afternoons the two young women went for a walk with Ethel's dog, Ella tall, boney, and large-mouthed, walked with a long stride, holding her head at a disdainful angle when anyone spoke to her. Ethel's more finely boned pale face, framed by her dark hair pulled evenly over both ears, would soften into an amused and sympathetic smile, her long thin mouth forming carefully chosen words, and speaking softly in a rather breathless, sad voice.

Christmas that year was full of foreboding. Vincent was no better, though he was only forty-nine. Ella was trying to hide the fact that she was hopelessly in love with a married man. Ethel had still failed to get herself published, and—a new cause for depression—Reggie had been sacked for intemperance at work. He hung about the house feeling a failure, fortifying himself in the dining room.

In January, 1901, Vincent resigned from the office. He was most generously granted a full salary for one more month, and then given an allowance of £400 a year to continue at the pleasure of the board of Governors. Obviously household spending had to be drastically reduced. First to go was the carriage and pair, to be replaced by a pony and trap for shopping. Reggie was offered a job by the Waldron Smithers in their family firm of Ackroyd and Smithers, stock jobbers in the City, which he gratefully accepted. He worked hard and soon rectified his previous lapse, confining any future drinking to when he was at home. Ella, who loved small children, started to teach some of her neighbours' offspring to read and write as well as to play the piano. For her own pleasure, and perhaps in order to find some way in which to express the emotions she was feeling, she learnt a lot of new and difficult songs, Duparc, Chausson, Ravel, and even Sibelius, accompanying herself as her voice rang out across and sometimes penetrated the shrine of her hopeless love. Waldron Smithers' wife had no idea of the anguish burning the soul of the eldest Dell girl. It probably never occurred to her that this awkward tall young woman was capable of any warm emotions. So Ella, keeping her anguish to herself, joined Smithers and his mother, a talented violinist, in playing trios—playing in fact with fire.

Sympathetic to a fault, Ethel alone knew the truth, and supported the weeping Ella in her arms night after night. It was, she must subconsciously have realised, wonderful copy, although at the time she would have been shocked to think that her sister's distress could be utilised in her writing.

Vincent allowed his daughters absolutely no pocket money. If they needed to buy something, they had to put it down in writing, leave it on his desk, and wait. Eventually there would be a long discussion held about the necessity for such extravagance. Vincent accompanied them whenever they went shopping, choosing their dresses himself. Ethel did not mind much, but for Ella, who had a love of rich colours and a flair for clothes, it was cruelly frustrating. Vincent was not going to have his daughters dressed in clothes that caught the eye, they must be modesty itself.

Ella never liked to buy clothes off the peg. If she was obliged to, they had to be altered slightly. A new set of buttons, a tuck here, a gay collar, or a binding on the hem, a habit that may well have begun with Vincent's parsimony. No clothes were ever long enough for her, so everything had to be lengthened. She was just on the six foot line.

Ethel's indifference to clothes was not surprising; she seemed to have no desire to go out and meet people. She was beginning to work long hours, getting up at four in the morning and writing to breakfast time, then again, if she felt fresh enough, until lunch. Although she was only twenty the creations of her brain were all the excitement she needed; she lived with them, suffering or rejoicing as they did. Her real world was on her carefully handwritten pages.

Ethel's interest in India had been stimulated by having younger cousins who had been born and brought up there. Her reading included the books of Flora Annie Steele, Maud Diver, Alice Perrin, and F. E. Penney. All these women writers were having their Indian Summer; with little to occupy their time while living in India, cossetted by servants and bored by their own company, they had been turning their hand to writing down their experiences. A flood of information was pouring out of India from the wives of army officers, civil servants, tea planters, and engineers. Most of it was good, solid, mediocre stuff, such as one would expect from intelligent but not conspicuously talented women, turning the commonplace intrigues of isolated up-country stations into romantic stories.

Ethel enjoyed searching through the writings of Rudyard Kipling, borrowing each book as it came out either from wealthier neighbours, or from Mudie's Library, from which she had a bundle of books every month.

She used these authors more for reference on habits, environment and custom than for their romantic appeal. Besides her short stories she was now embarking on her first full-scale novel. Her first acceptances were by editors of magazines devoted exclusively to romance. Many of these were being published at that time, intended especially for women with tiring and monotonous jobs; housekeepers, governesses, lady companions, maids, nurses, the sad and the bored.

That Ethel never aimed her cultural sights higher was not due to any lack of education, since, like her sister, she was well-read and cultured. Her sympathies, however, were with those who were forced to work in uncongenial jobs; to them she set out to bring glamour and excitement.

She told stories that were not beyond their understanding; of situations in which it would be marvellous for them to find themselves, a viable dream world. Her characters were those with whom such readers could identify; her themes were plausible, and, best of all, the reader was led, from the very first line, from one exciting emotional situation to the next, full of action with love scenes that, though 'hot', were morally acceptable.

The difficulties she encountered before first getting a novel published seem now almost incredible. Ella supported her wholeheartedly, in return for Ethel's constant sympathy, spending all the time that she was not practising or teaching in typing out 'Nettie's' stories, finding publishers to send them to, and when they came back scuffed, patiently typing them all out again. Vincent never ceased to be encouraging. He was proud of his younger daughter, though he did not understand her. He knew she was a good girl, with impeccable morals, but where had she learnt all this 'love tosh'? Irene, who had much more imagination, understood her better.

On 2nd December, 1901, the Literary Agents, Pinker and Co. received a letter from Ethel.

> Elgin House,
> Knockholt,
> Kent.

Sir,
  I have been recommended to write to you by the editor of the *Royal*.
  I should be glad if you would let me know your terms for disposing of a novel to a publishers.
  Awaiting your reply.

> Yours faithfully,
> E. M. Dell

No wasting of words, brief and to the point. Ella, with her practical common sense may have helped with the draft. Ethel did not have long to wait for a reply, the post was better in those days. Her next letter written only two days later, was a little less formal, but quite firm.

> Elgin House,
> Knockholt,
> Kent.

Dear Sir,
  I am in receipt of your letter. I am willing to accept your terms, and am forwarding my MSS'S for your perusal.

I must mention that before I was recommended to write to you, I sent three stories to F. V. White and Co., Publishers, Bedford Street, who would have published them but I did not consider their terms sufficiently tempting.

I then sent the third of them (*The Hon. Burford*) to the Editor of the *Royal*, who returned it as unsuitable for that magazine, and advised me to write to you.

I should like the stories to appear in the order in which they are numbered and under the title of the first.

Yours faithfully,
E. M. Dell

So, all at once, Ethel is accepted, turns down the money as not sufficient, and rather than argue about the matter in an unlady-like way, puts all her work in the hands of an agent. V. F. White and Co., must have chewed off their knuckles when at a much later date Ethel's sales began to soar.

It is not hard to imagine the two girls' excitement, Ella delighted that at last beloved Nettie was being taken seriously. Messrs. Pinker, in the meantime, obviously considered her stories worth trying with a publisher as they wrote again on the 8th December asking for her ideas as to their grouping. Ethel replied on the 10th December.

Elgin House,
Knockholt,
Kent.

Dear Sir,

My idea for the three stories which I sent you was that they should be published together in one volume (say a three shilling book) entitled *Bristles* (the title of the first story). I cannot condense them without spoiling them.

As to the agreement, I now have two short stories accepted by the *Universal and Ludgate Magazine*, which have not yet been published, and he has expressed his willingness to consider any short stories I may send him. I therefore am not disposed to give up that opening.

Otherwise I would put all my work through your hands.

I shall be glad to hear from you on these points.

Yours faithfully,
E. M. Dell

The agreement does not say that I am to be consulted with regard to the terms upon which my work is taken by a publisher, but I suppose that would be so.

One can imagine the girls putting their heads together determined not to be 'done' by a mere agent, and a man. The last sentence sounds like Ella.

During 1902 Ethel wrote some stories which were accepted and serialised in the *Red Magazine,* and was working on her first novel. Perhaps the fact that the *Universal and Ludgate Magazine* had accepted her work was encouragement enough to set her to work on a full-length book. The *Ludgate* had a very different class of reader to the *Royal.* This would have pleased Ella who was inclined towards intellectual snobbery. She did not really care for her sister's writing, but was so determined that Nettie's feelings should not be hurt, that she kept her judgment to herself. Given to reading Goethe in the original German, Verlaine poems which had not yet been translated, and quoting Ruskin, Ella was a daunting young women to talk to. Yet she had a rare gift for inspiring children to make the most of their brains; her enthusiastic approach to learning was infectious. Ella could make bright children precociously brilliant, parents began to seek her out.

Yet Ella was restless. She lacked Ethel's inner resources and was more of an extrovert, loving brilliant colours and the rich music of Brahms, Debussy, Beethoven, and Chopin, preferably to be performed by herself and before a sympathetic audience.

Both young women had passionate natures. But while Ethel expressed hers privately, Ella needed the complement of a husband, and she knew this only too well. But her chances of meeting men were limited, particularly as what she would need was one who was at least six feet three inches tall, musical, and intelligent enough to talk interestingly. She knew it was highly unlikely that such a paragon would ever come her way. So, as best she could, she masked her shyness with a big hearty laugh. Often, in private, it turned to tears.

FIVE

1903-1909

IN 1903 a new family arrived in Knockholt. Cecil A. V. Bowra and his wife and two sons took Highmanswick, not far from Elgin House. They were home on leave from China where Cecil Bowra held a post in the Chinese Customs Service. They were to be in England for a year, with their sons, aged six and seven. Having been babies when they left England, they now spoke fluent Cantonese, and enough Russian to be cheeky to the Russian soldiers who guarded the next door compound in Peking. Mrs. Bowra had taught the boys to read and write; they had begun to explore the avenues of English history, and could both say their times tables. They badly needed a governess; Ella was recommended. Edward and Maurice took to her at once. She had a knack of treating children as her equals, so they felt they could tell her anything, admit ignorance, or even show off without being laughed at or told to behave. Ella was immediately fascinated by 'The Bowra boys', as she always referred to them, even when they were in their late fifties. Edward was shy and studious, Maurice perky and extremely quick and amusing. That Maurice preferred to stand on his head in an arm chair while repeating the story of the battle of Thermopylae, is credit to Ella that she let him be himself. They loved Ella and learnt fast from her. She in turn became totally devoted to them, channelling most of her energy into finding new and interesting subjects to teach them. She was much happier, and probably spent less time projecting her soulful contralto over the road.

Maurice Bowra in his *Memories* remarked, 'Of course I was spoiled, it was well worth it, and I have nothing but gratitude for those who did it.' This may well have included Ella.

Twice a year 'ugly' Aunt May Dell and her dapper brother William came to spend a fortnight at Elgin House. Vincent enjoyed these visits greatly. Although they were sad about his slip from faith, they were not censorious. On Sundays, when fit enough himself, he would drive them seven miles to the nearest Catholic church while the rest of the family went to the Protestant service in Knockholt.

Vincent's niece, now Dame Joan McLaughlin, remembers his kindness to her, when, as a small child aged seven years, she went to stay on her own with the Dells at Knockholt. Strictly brought up by her mother, Vincent's sister, and her father—an Irishman with the blood of St. Patrick O'Toule running in his veins, she was already a stickler for Catholic procedure. When Sunday came round it seemed too far and too much trouble to drive a small girl seven miles to church on her own, so she took the situation into her own hands and read through the entire service aloud in the dining room, and to reinforce the nature of the exercise, chose to read it in the Latin version. It was done in what she now calls a deliberate desire to irritate.

Ella heard her, came into the room, and threw up her hands in horror. 'What idiotic rubbish are you gabbling, and what good *do* you think it will do you?' There was no reply, only a sweet smile; one suspects Joan had the same determined attitude to opposition as Ella. Vincent who was passing, told Ella to leave the child alone. Ethel's policy of non-interference was remembered by Joan with gratitude. She was 'gentle, sweet, kind, and never cross'.

When Joan was in her teens, and a pupil at Oulton Abbey, Ethel sent her copies of *Sunday Stories*, possibly in the hope that she would not end her days as a nun. Joan read these one Sunday afternoon in the Abbey gardens, and came in pink-cheeked and bright-eyed. The nuns were shocked and tried to make her promise not to read them. In spite of these distractions Dame Joan has spent all her life as an enclosed nun at Stanbrook Abbey, and still has bright eyes, and pink cheeks. She does not seem to have missed anything in life outside.

Ethel's stories were now beginning to be read by members of her family. Joan's older brothers had an embarrassing moment when Vincent arrived unexpectedly to see their mother. They were reading Ethel's latest instalment in the *Red Book*, shrieking with delight as they counted up the number of times she had used the words 'passion, tremble, pant, thrill' and marking the pages with a pencil. Vincent, hearing the laughter, put his head around the door. 'What are you up to?' he asked. There was a nasty silence, he walked into the room and picked up the magazine, saw the pencil marks and realised at once what they represented.

With an enormous grin he said 'There are two more "trembles" a few pages further on.' The McLaughlin boys' relief can be imagined.

Vincent's variable health continued to disrupt the family peace. As his tempers became increasingly choleric, only Ella could handle his moods. Irene made no attempt to help, keeping herself apart from any possibility of loud-mouthed encounters with her husband, and seeing as little of him as she could. Ethel worried continually about her 'dear little mother'.

Ethel's novel was progressing slowly. She had an excellent plot, but did not know how to link it together without obvious breaks. The bagpipes, it might be said, were blowing wildly, but the drone could not be heard. Her writing technique needed to be improved, but to whom could she turn? Certainly Ella could be of no help; her austere prose would have killed Ethel's style, and it is to Ella's credit that, apart from spelling and grammatical howlers, she never attempted to influence Ethel.

The year 1907 saw big changes in the Dell household. Vincent's gout grew so much worse it was decided to move to another house, where medical aid would be more easily available. Ella was allotted the task of finding a new home, which gave her a welcome opportunity to exercise her organising powers. She put her whole mind to the job, and eventually discovered a suitable house in Ashford, Middlesex, not far from the Thames. Although in a much more built-up area than Knockholt, it was still in those days in the country. There were lovely lanes to explore on bicycles, yet it was within easy walk of good shops. Above all there were doctors and a hospital; Ella felt it might not be long before Vincent would need specialist care.

Chattern House was no smaller than Elgin House, but it had less land, no tennis court and only small stables, enough for a pony and trap. A great improvement for them all, and even if a heart had been left behind, the proximity and frustration were eased. There was an excellent train service to London if needed, and Knockholt and their friends were only twenty odd miles away.

Here their first new acquaintances were the Vidlers. Dr. Vidler became a firm friend as well as medical adviser. Evelyn, their daughter, although a little younger, struck a good friendship with Ella. She was round-faced, plump, had titian hair, was full of fun and had many suitors to spare.

Ethel had by now finished the fourth or fifth draft of her first novel, and let Pinker have it. He did his best but was quite unable to place it. Ethel had begun her 'journey in the desert'.

Ella never failed to open her arms to comfort the weeping Ethel, and uncomplainingly re-typed the manuscript whenever it became too worn. No one on those days had the temerity to publish a book of this sort written by a woman. Perhaps the publishers to whom it was shown were nervous of the criticism it was bound to bring in. No publisher worth the paper he printed on wished to be associated with really popular reading. Even now, when Ethel has been dead for nearly forty years, a publisher when questioned about her early books, remarked 'Oh surely we did not have anything to do with *her*, did we?' There was a curious feeling of polite distaste, an antiseptic washing of the hands.

When they moved to Chattern House, Ethel was in her twenty-sixth year, and Ella nearly twenty nine. They were already beginning to settle into spinsterish ways, taking regular timed walks with Ethel's dog every afternoon; people could set clocks by their passing. Ella joined the local choir, and sang the St. Matthew Passion at Easter. Ethel continued to be woken up by her dog at four every morning, working through until breakfast; she lost weight and began to look drawn. Ella would take her up hot milk at night. They sat on her bed together in dressing gowns, viewing the future gloomily, arms round each other's shoulders. There was not much laughter, and a considerable amount of sadness. Sometimes Ella would cuddle round Ethel until she fell asleep, then creep out of the room and silently glide back to her own cold bed. There was always the fear of disturbing Vincent and precipitating a rampage.

Occasionally Ella went up to London, for concerts, which gave her great pleasure and something on which to feed her hungry mind. She heard Adelina Patti, whom she described as 'very swoopy', Caruso 'He took my breath away', Melba, 'getting old'. The Albert Hall once heard her own voice when the Ashford choir was one of those which sang Bach's Christmas Oratoria. Her only comment: 'The acoustics are atrocious'.

Ella now taught singing as well as the piano, but did little other teaching; the Bowra boys had spoilt her for mediocre minds, and were now in China.

With Ethel's acceptances, Ella's teaching and Vincent's pension, they were solvent. Vincent, however, still refused to let them wear clothes that they had bought without consulting him, disparagingly suggesting that such garments would do for the church bazaar.

Ashford Public Library was a great source of joy to them; Ethel used often to bicycle in and do research, bringing back a bundle of books in her wickerwork handlebar basket. Ella would accompany her to do some shopping, and in summer they would take the long way home round Staines Reservoir, partly because it was very pretty, and also hoping to see some cars on the main road south out of London.

Ethel was totally entranced with their shape and smell, sound, and above all the 'swift movement' of cars. How she longed to ride in one, but so far the nearest had been a bus ride down Park Lane after going to a concert at the Wigmore Hall with Ella. They had travelled on the top, enthroned as if in a howdah, with waterproof aprons fixed over their knees. They had held hands beneath this covering, squeezing their fingers in excitement every time the bus stopped or started. When they reached home there was no enthusiast to whom they could ascribe their adventure; Vincent growled that horses were safer and cheaper, and Irene, 'dear little Mother', gently agreed, too nervous to cross her husband.

Dr. Vidler suggested that Vincent would benefit from a little sea air, so Ella took him for a week to Bognor. When it was fine, she pushed him along the front in a bath chair. He enjoyed it and grew much better tempered. Ella recalled that she got closer to him on these trips, which became regular, than she had ever hoped. They talked into the early hours, discussing their frustrated ambitions and managing a little sympathy for each other. Ethel also benefited as she had Irene to herself and they gossiped over the drawing room fire at tea-time. Without the

intimidating presence of Vincent, Irene was able to be herself.
They talked of disappointments, Irene assuring Ethel that, as a
young man, her father had been quite different, while Ethel
wondered why her novel had not been acclaimed. Fortunately
she was unaware that it so far had been declined by no fewer
than five publishers. Still full of confidence, she was now well
into her second book. It is not known now what titles she originally gave these two first novels. Eventually they became famous
as *The Way of an Eagle*, followed by *The Knave of Diamonds*.
Ella's own efforts in typing and retyping them were never forgotten either by herself or by a grateful Ethel.

Ethel had a phenomenal memory and could accurately
describe people she had met from all walks in life, ever since
childhood. She remembered what they looked like, the colour of
their eyes and hair, the way they walked, their views on politics,
how they dressed as distinct from what they wore, and, un-
failingly, their names. She was never too busy to stop and talk
to people, the postman, the plumber, the baker, the gardener,
shop assistants, even dustmen. Children, though, embarrassed
her, she lacked Ella's gift for putting them at ease.

People liked telling Ethel their troubles; she 'listened', they
said, with such a sweet smile, and was 'so sympathetic', and
later, 'so generous'. As Vincent had by now begun to refuse to
allow any visitors to come to the house, any excitements had to
be found elsewhere. For Ethel these chance meetings were more
than enough to keep her happily writing until dawn, her mental
bread and butter being supplied by everyday encounters aided
by a catholic choice of daily newspapers for which she paid herself, Vincent groaning that they were ridiculously expensive.
He was not averse, however, to reading them when Ethel had
finished, enjoying a grumble over the disgusting way young
people behaved.

The Bowras had been back in Peking several years but were
due to return on leave in 1910. Ella kept up correspondence
with them and sent the boys books, keeping an eye open for new
and stimulating reading. Her love of poetry and the classics
must obviously have had some small part in aiming Maurice in
the direction in which he was to excel.

The boys' letters to her were magical, from a world totally
beyond her own experience. She encouraged them to describe

everything, partly to stimulate their powers of observation, and also to bring China right into her own life. How she longed to experience it all, the Great Wall, the rancid stink as the muleteers passed by with their chow dogs, to hear temple gongs, eat rice with chopsticks, see women hobbling on bound feet, and handle fine porcelain in the shops.

Secondhand experience may have sufficed for Ethel; it was fearful for Ella, who pined for reality.

As the years passed, it was clear that the Bowra boys would have to go to an English public school. But would they be able to sit for their entrance exam? By 1909 they had one year left to do some cramming while still in China, Edward was twelve and Maurice eleven. Mr. Bowra wrote to Vincent Dell.

Ella found his letter on the door mat and with trembling hands took it up to her father, who grumpily opened it, read a few words, then told her to go downstairs, it was none of her business. Ella knew very well who the letter came from and that it must refer to her. When they were last on leave, Mrs. Bowra had mentioned in a vague way that it would be nice if Ella could accompany them back to China as governess to the two boys, but no more had been said. Three years had passed.

Vincent did not mention the letter again until Ella, in desperation, several days later asked him what it had been about. Then; 'You had better read it yourself, but don't entertain any ideas that you can go to them. I would never give my permission for you to leave this country.' Ella read the letter and it was as she suspected—an invitation from the Bowras to go out as companion governess to them in Peking, asking her father's permission and blessing, as Maurice and Edward loved her, and now needed a little intelligent tutoring.

This was the opportunity of a lifetime, Ella had an adventurous spirit, her home life was dull and monotonous. Ella longed to spread her wings, her own pet expression. Perhaps in far-off Peking she could find, amongst the international society that lived there, a suitable life companion, even someone tall *and* intelligent.

Proud Ella became the humble beggar, imploring her father to let her go. She went down on her knees to him in his study, she wept, she argued, she even threatened to run away to China when persuasion failed. Vincent was totally unyielding, he needed her to run the house while Ethel did her writing, and someone must take care of him, and, of course, of Irene! 'It is your duty to stay here and look after us,' he shouted. 'You should be ashamed of yourself for entertaining for one moment the thought of leaving us old people, after all we have done for you.'

That was the end of any hope. Ella never forgave her father, and privately hated him until he died. She felt he had been deliberately selfish and although, as far as he was concerned, carried out her duties meticulously, it was with a hard heart. She no longer sympathised with his foul tempers, and simply ignored his petulant behaviour. Yet when he raged, and was at his worst, she alone could control him.

Not only did Ella never forgive her father; she never forgot the missed opportunity. If she was depressed, as happened fairly frequently in old age, she would walk up and down the room, saying, 'He should have let me go, it was so *mean*'. Only very close relatives knew to what she was referring.

SIX

The Way of an Eagle

BETWEEN 1910 and 1912, Ethel's novel, *The Way of an Eagle*, was refused by eight publishers. It changed its shape and length several times but never its essential plot, despite kindly but superfluous advice from Ella, Reggie and the Vidler family, her agent having become rather bored. Ethel never altered the core of the story, so confident was she that it was good. All it needed was the right reader, she was convinced.

T. Fisher Unwin was publishing a 'First Novel Library' to which the reading public were accustomed to looking for new authors. It is also to his credit that he ran one of the first prize competitions for novels by unknown writers.

In 1911 Ethel submitted her typescript, and amongst the many hundreds that arrived hers was recognised as very possible material, although it was at this time some 300,000 words long. Ethel did not win the prize, but was given sound advice and suggestions for improvement. Overjoyed, she worked hard at the story yet again, and after many journeys to and fro in the post, each time for yet another adjustment, and still more typing for Ella, it was reduced to 90,000 words and accepted.

T. Fisher Unwin thought that they had a best seller, but could not have anticipated the enormous success it was to enjoy. *The Way* as it was called in the family, came out in January 1912, when Ethel was 31, and Ella within a few days of her 34th birthday. It had been a very long fight to win, the girls were almost middle-aged, certainly in habit, but still looked rather untouched by reality. Reggie took Ethel's picture to celebrate the day. She wore a neat white blouse, heavy skirt, sensible shoes, and her expression, although a little strained, perhaps by much writing in a bad light, seems only half aware. There is no flowering maturity in the look of pleased disbelief she gave him, as she sat on a kitchen chair in the orchard at Ashford.

The sales of *Way of an Eagle* outstripped the publishers' wildest dreams. Between 1912 and 1915 it went through no less than 27 printings, each larger than the one before. Ethel, though she was unaware of it at the time, was responsible for half T. Fisher Unwin's hardly inconsiderable turnover.

Vincent was absolutely bowled over with pride, so much so that Ella showed a distinct tendency towards jealously: Ethel might be 'made', but Ella, still with no definite aim in life, became torn with conflicting emotions. Enchanted that her darling Nettie was at last famous, she longed for recognition of some sort for herself. Irene saw how unhappy Ella was, and diplomatically suggested that she should take Vincent off to Bognor again for a week or so to recover from all the excitement. But it was to be over a year before they eventually got away together. As Ethel's most willing but unpaid slave, Ella now had to help with fan mail, as well as alterations to *The Knave of Diamonds*, which Unwin were by now demanding.

In the spring of 1913 Ella and Vincent arrived once more at Bognor, but for the last time. Vincent had a stroke, and died after only a few days at the seaside. Ella was greatly shocked, she had not seen death before. But with her usual ability to organise, she arranged for Vincent's body to be taken home by train; the coffin travelled in the guard's van and she sat in a compartment as near to it as she could. At Ashford they were met by the undertakers, in whose funeral parlour he lay until his burial.

Irene could not bring herself to go and see him, but Ella, Ethel and Reggie, bade their last farewells to him there. Ella remembered Ethel being white-faced, dry-eyed and tight-lipped, Reggie sadly flippant, thoroughly nervous and making small jokes in his hesitant high-pitched voice.

Ella herself was too busy arranging wreaths, relatives and refreshments to realise that she was at last free of his heavy harness until several weeks after the funeral, to which all the living Dells and Parrotts came, the latter perfectly satisfied at the arrangements, the former horrified that Vincent had not been given the last rites, nor returned to his Catholic fold.

Although Irene and Vincent had never shown each other much public demonstrable affection, there must have been a life partnership of considerable tenacity. Irene now slowly retreated into old age and ill health; never a very warm personality, she withdrew into icy silences.

Ethel's first substantial earnings were spent in a present to Ella and Reggie, a lump sum to be spent on travel, her only stipulation. It was not enough to take them to China, but even so, Ella's excitement can be imagined. They went to Thomas Cooks and were advised to go to Switzerland. With the enthusiasm of children released from parental restriction they bought Baedekers, boots, skates, scarves, woolly gloves and hats. Ella read every helpful book she could find, they bought a camera and borrowed binoculars. nothing was forgotten. Their holiday was a magic enchantment, the first escape from England. They both enjoyed themselves thoroughly as, apart from scenery and good food, they met the Philips family, whose daughters were to play a lasting role in the Dells' lives.

Ethel soon began to earn considerable sums of money. Her first big buy was a black Daimler, which she called Martha, who arrived complete with chauffeur. This extravagance was not primarily for herself, but for her mother. She was greatly disappointed that Martha had not arrived in time to give her father pleasure. People still remember the sight of old Mrs. Dell, sitting stiffly upright in the back of the big black car, small but dignified, with her gloved hands closed together on her rug-wrapped lap, and nodding faintly at acquaintances as the Daimler slowly rolled by.

By 1914 Irene was a sick woman, the Great War was boiling up on the horizon, and Reggie had joined the Territorials. He enjoyed spending most weekends training, and was beginning to take a serious interest in women. Ethel's *The Knave of Diamonds* was published, and sold out immediately. Money began to roll in and she gave Reggie and Ella large allowances. Reggie spent his on wine, woman and good living; Ella bought herself a Broadway grand piano, and patronised Debenham and Freebody's, where she found just the sort of clothes she had always longed for, and, oh, such splendid hats.

August arrived and with it the War. Reggie was called up at once, Ella trained to be a V.A.D. Nurse and exchanged her lovely new clothes for a nurse's uniform. There was a Hospital near Ashford which had been turned into a recuperating centre for Officers where she put in several half-days a week. Irene

could not be left for long, so full-time work was impossible.
Ethel, who had never been very 'robust', a word much used in
the Dell house, was unable to lift her mother in and out of bed,
yet Irene refused to have paid help, being too shy to admit her
wants to a stranger. Dr. Vidler cared for her assiduously, calling
nearly every day, and his daughter, Evelyn, already a great
friend of the family, came in to sit with Irene when Ella was out
at her Hospital. Ethel did not alter her own way of life at all, not
through selfishness, but because her public were demanding
more books, and she felt it her duty to give pleasure to others.
Her sudden wealth was an embarrassment to her, she could only
feel comfortable if she gave it away.

One joy, recorded by camera, was a visit by the Philips girls,
who brought their youngest sister Patsie with them. While
they were staying at Chattern House, Reggie arrived on leave.
He was about to be sent to Gallipoli. Fortunately soldiers do not
know what lies ahead; in the photograph he looks happy, if thin
and tired. Ella completes the picture with Jimmy sitting near, a
self-contained little dog. That Ethel seldom appears in these
early pictures confirms her refusal to be photographed. She was
not just shy, it was an almost paranoiac desire for physical
anonymity, except when forced by her own family, as on the day
of the publication of her first book. Any pictures taken after
that were obtained only with great difficulty and much persuasion. The Press never did get one.

It has been said that she deliberately wound a veil of mystery
about herself to add glamour to her books. This is most unlikely; much more probably Ethel was two people, the writer
who was bold, and the real person who was shy. For them to
meet on common ground would have destroyed her dream
world, and been contrary to her personality.

Sometime during 1915 a red haired young woman came to
live in Ashford, a proud and fiery character who refused any help
although she had a red haired baby daughter to bring up, her
husband having deserted her. Mrs. Talbot was a trained nurse,
and soon found work helping out Dr. Vidler with his bedridden
patients, much as a district nurse would, dropping in to do
dressings, and give bed-baths. Dr. Vidler knew she would be an
invaluable help to the Dells, and after discussion with them,
Ella set off in Martha with the chauffeur to find her tiny cottage,

and ask her if she would consider coming to them as a permanent nurse for Irene. In Mrs. Talbot's own words: 'I took one look at that hoity toity big woman standing there and I said to myself, no, not for all the tea in China.' She then politely but firmly refused on the ground that it would mean putting Peggy, her daughter, into family care. Ella tried persuasion in vain.

Some months later she buried her pride and tried again, Irene now needed constant attention, but the answer was the same, and she was forced to give up nursing officers, which she had rather enjoyed, even though, as she put it, some of them were temporary gentlemen. It was about now, with enough money to do more than 'keep up', that Ella began to wriggle out of her solid middle-class background and reach for the upper echelons of society.

By 1916 Irene was suffering from high blood pressure. Dr. Vidler recommended leeches but Ella could not bring herself to place them on her mother's body, while Ethel, writing as usual, could do no night nursing at all. Ella was becoming exhausted, and had taken to long bouts of weeping. Ethel asked Dr. Vidler where Mrs. Talbot lived, and as it was not far, walked there. Finding her in the garden hanging up washing, she asked her very gently if she could possibly change her mind and come as a full-time nurse. Mrs. Talbot took another look, dropped everything, except baby Peggy who was tucked under her arm and returned immediately with Ethel. Thus Nursie joined the Dell household. She adored Ethel, saying she was a darling, with a sense of humour, also retiring, religious, and with an extraordinary ability to teach dogs complicated tricks. About Ella, Nursie was less enthusiastic. 'She was haughty, inclined to overdress, gave an unprepossessing impression, stand-offish, and never let her hair down. It was for Miss Ethel that I bore Miss Ella.'

Yet Ella so longed to be loved, she ached with loneliness, and to hide her hurt she adopted a guarded manner with anyone she did not know well, hence Nursie's remark—stand-offish. Peggy came to live in the house, and this gave Ella an idea, one which at this stage she handled somewhat clumsily. She would offer to adopt her—but first she must ask Irene what she thought about it. Waiting until her mother had a better day, she broached the subject. There was a long silence, Ella thought that she could

not have heard, and was about to explain further, when Irene
turned her head on the pillow and said, 'No daughter of mine
shall have or adopt a child out of wedlock. Only married women
with children are acceptable in society.' So that idea came to an
abrupt end. Nursie knew nothing of what might have been
blowing in the wind. In any case she would never have agreed.

Almost the most important inhabitant in the house was
Ethel's little border terrier Jimmy. Ethel certainly considered
him to be as near human as any dog could become, and treated
him accordingly. He had great personality and there was
amazing rapport between them. Jimmy was a small, black,
rough-haired dog with light moustaches and eyebrows. He had
entered the house as a puppy when they moved to Ashford in
1907, and became Ethel's companion and shadow, with a
definite job of work to do. He slept in a basket in her bedroom,
and had been taught, by means unknown, to wake Ethel at four
o'clock each morning by jumping on her bed and licking her
face. Ethel would get up and start her writing, Jimmy would
trundle back to his basket and sleep, but should anyone try
Ethel's door or even pause outside, he would wake and give a
spine-chilling growl.

That Ethel managed to write so much so fast, must in some
measure have been due to Jimmy. Her output was astonishing,
even given the fact that much of it had begun before she first
achieved publication. In the five years from 1912 to 1917, she
completed nine books, all of which were published. They
appeared in the following order: *The Way of an Eagle, The
Knave of Diamonds, The Swindler, The Desire of his Life,
The Rocks of Valpre, The Keeper of the Door, The Bars of Iron,
The Hundredth Chance,* and a collection of three stories entitled
The Safety Curtain.

If only for his part in this great effort, Jimmy deserved the
honourable place he was given in the family, the best food,
regular walks, and plenty of attention—in Ethel's case much
cuddling. That he was intelligent there is no doubt, he could
walk on his hind legs balancing a lump of sugar on his nose, and
was an enthusiastic participant in games of hunt-the-thimble.
It was not necessary to hide the thimble where he could smell it;
even if it was balanced on a picture rail, he would see it, point
with his nose and bark excitedly.

In May 1918 Irene died, Nursie's efforts had undoubtedly prolonged her life by at least two years. Ethel was desolate, and for weeks seemed inconsolable. Composing poetry and blank verse, mostly addressed to her dead mother, she let her normal writing slide to a stop, taking Jimmy for long walks, and re-reading her fan mail as if searching for comfort.

Ella missed her mother too, but having a more practical mind, and being made of sterner fibre, she realised that she now truly had freedom to do as she liked. She was thirty-eight, and had again been nursing at the Officers' Hospital regularly since Nursie had taken charge of her mother. Some of her gaucherie had worn off, she was not nearly so awkward in the presence of men, and could now recount an anecdote without blushing self-consciously. Love had not come her way, but a degree of self-assurance.

One such story of Ella's is worth recalling.

Ella was on duty in the hospital when a new patient arrived. He had been very badly wounded and shell shocked, and although ostensibly better, the hospital being for rehabilitation, he looked a ghastly colour and was utterly limp, giving little groans and fluttering his eyelids. Ella saw him into bed, took his temperature and pulse, which were quite normal, and asked him if he would like anything to eat or drink.

'Ah . . ., dear Nurse, he replied, 'Oh, for a drink of the waters of Lethe.'

Ella knew immediately what he meant, though she was not sure whether his affectation amused or annoyed her. With an effort she kept a smile from her face, when a voice from the bed next door called out.

'How about a bottle of Perrier water . . . that might help, I am sure Nurse would get it for you.'

Could he have been one of Ella's temporary gentlemen, or a gentleman deliberately feigning ignorance? Did Ella always know the difference?

SEVEN

Wealth and Woe

ETHEL'S DEAREST companions were all women possessing dominant characters, kind, firm, protective, and apt to be jealous of one another. Of this she was probably not aware, or if she was, would certainly not have used the situation to set them against each other, as a less responsible or malicious woman might. She disliked causing discomfort to others, and saw herself as a peacemaker and benefactor. Devoting her life to living out her principals, she was never known to have lost her temper, used bad language, spoken harshly or behaved selfishly. Perhaps surprisingly, though, she was no prudish saint. Infinitely sweet and gently funny, she could be witty without malice. Her intellectual reading level ruled out sharing many of Ella's thoughts or friends, and it may have been her lack of desire to express her outlook on life through her writing except in overt acts by her characters, which led her towards women friends of masculine type who acted rather than thought. None of them ever married.

Ethel's friends thought they understood her, enjoyed her books, talked to her about them and asked for more. The heterosexually inexperienced woman fitted, she had no right to criticise the validity of Ethel's emotional extravaganzas; she was not supposed to know anyway, and was only to happy to accept what she read and enjoy it.

The Way of an Eagle brought Ethel her first fan mail, and her first friendship outside the family circle. So many admirers wrote letters when her book came out that she was overwhelmed and embarrassed, instinctively retreating from this pile of paper ululations. Yet she felt she must read them all, a mixed feeling of incredulity that she should cause so widespread a reaction, and pleasure that so many lonely people had been touched and warmed, encouraged her to answer every letter that gave an address. Amongst these was a Miss Cassan, a spinster of Ethel's own age, who lived with an ageing mother in Guildford.

A devoted daughter tied to duty, an avid reader of escapist novels, and a thoroughly kind, firm, loyal woman, she had long since given up any thought of marriage. Ethel's sympathies were always with the underprivileged, the loser, and the selfless soul who forgot herself in doing good for others. Miss Cassan fitted into this last category. They wrote, they met and became firm friends, much to Ella's annoyance, who referred to her as 'that Cassan woman'.

With both parents dead, the sisters were free to move to a better house. Ethel was now earning vast sums of money, somewhere in the region of £20,000 a year, and tax in those days was negligible. She expressed a desire to live near Miss Cassan, which must have been galling for Ella, but Ethel had the money, she could call the tune, and did so. Miss Cassan wrote to tell them that there was a very large and pleasant house called The Greenwood for sale, only a few minutes' walk away from her home. Ethel and Ella drove over in Martha, liked the house, and bought it.

'Little Mother' Irene had been dead only a few months when they moved. Ethel was missing her intensely; there was a gap in her life that needed filling and the Cassan friendship began to flourish.

Ethel took two weeks off every year to have a holiday. That year she invited 'The Cassan' to join her. Ella was left behind to see to decorating the new house, a job which appealed to her very much, particularly as money was no object. Taking the chauffeur and Martha, Ethel and Miss Cassan set off for the west country, staying in hotels where they signed the register in each other's names. Already Ethel was suffering from too much attention from the Press, they dogged her footsteps and made life miserable.

Miss Cassan thoroughly enjoyed the experience of being tailed by journalists, then refusing to say anything or to be photographed, Ethel had a relatively peaceful holiday except for one incident. She locked herself in the lavatory and could not get out. Far too shy to call out, she struggled with the lock until exhausted, then quietly waited to be found.

Miss Cassan was frantic, looking for her all over the hotel and gardens, sending porters and maids to search for her. Eventually, going to 'pay a visit', as they would have said, before renewing her efforts, she found the door locked, rattled it and was about to walk off when she heard a small voice say 'Is that you, Cassie darling?' Ethel was eventually released by a carpenter. Blushing with embarrassment she rushed to her room, packed her things and ordered the car. Rather than face the amused and sympathetic smiles of the management she put a hundred miles between herself and them by nightfall.

Nursie was not then in her employment, but once when Miss Cassan was ill, Ethel sent for her, and insisted that she should nurse her until she was cured, a procedure which annoyed both Miss Cassan and Nursie, as one was not ill enough and the other thought her a frump. 'Ever so ugly, she was, had a moustache.' Perhaps, but it is surprising how dislike can breed inaccuracies, particularly of personal looks. It is also a prime example of the type of jealously which seemed to pervade all Ethel's friends, a rather sour dislike of each other.

Another very dear friend, also first discovered in her fan mail, was also a spinster with an elderly mother at home. Violet Ebsworth, was a secretary to one of the big publishers. Unlike Miss Cassan, she was small and neat, with sharp dark eyes. She could ruffle and shake herself, like a blackbird after a bath, if annoyed, but like Ethel she eschewed strong words. To Ethel's delight, she had first written in sympathy for one of her heroines, a correspondence started, and then Violet very shyly suggested helping her with her fan mail which was becoming mountainous. They met for lunch in London, liked each other instantaneously and Violet was invited for a weekend at the Greenwood. Ethel felt that she should see for herself the amount of work involved, fan mail is also very personal, only someone in complete sympathy could have been allowed to read it.

Violet was astonished. The postman delivered a sack of letters every day. Wondering how Ethel could possibly have had time to read them all, let alone answer them, she took a closer look at her, and realised that her hostess, unselfishly trying to cope by herself, was thin, her eyes were ringed with dark, and her hands trembled. Violet's first thought was for Ethel, and being a determined little woman, she persuaded her that it was ridiculous to waste her energies on her readers if she was going to be too tired to write for them. Ethel succumbed gratefully. Violet gave up her job in London, her home in Basingstoke was not too far away, so it was arranged that Ethel should first read her mail, then send it over in Martha with appropriate comments for Violet to type the answers, then once a week Violet returned in Martha to the Greenwood, had lunch with Ethel and Ella, and then settled down to putting the answers in envelopes.

Although this arrangement was on a business footing, Ethel and Violet became fond of one another. Ella, too found Violet delightful. Her quick wit and her astonishing ability to recite nearly all of Edward Lear's Nonsense Poems, in a growly voice, made them look forward to her visits.

That Ella had never seriously taken on Ethel's letters was not surprising, she was intensely jealous of anyone winning Ethel's attention or affection. Ethel had to tread like Agag in the vicinity of Ella's feelings. It is a measure of Violet's tact that both sisters were able to like her openly.

Violet's brother Cyril, a very tall shy man, also made his appearance as the friendship grew, distantly falling in love with Ella, but never daring to propose. She had so much money now, there was little he could offer her, yet had he known that affection was all she really needed, he might well have been emboldened to risk it. They wrote regularly to each other on the first of the month, a coolly affectionate correspondence that lasted all their lives.

Ella had kept in touch with the Bowra boys. By now they were young men, and had left Cheltenham, Edward was a serving officer, and Maurice had been sent back to China to fill in time, being too young to be called up. Before Maurice left Cheltenham and when he still had his Oxford Scholarship exams in front of him, he wrote to Ella the following letter, sending her at the same time a copy of Swinburne's *Atalanta in Calydon*. He was just seventeen.

Cheltondale,
Cheltenham,
Nov: 5th.

Dear Miss Dell,
Herewith the *Atalanta*. I am sorry not to have sent it before but this week I have been whirled off my feet with

multitudinous duties and have not had a moment to myself today.

I hope that you will like the play. Please note the opening chorus. Althaea's long speeches, the blasphemous chorus in the style of Ezekiel (a wonderful piece of music) and the last lyrical digs between Meleager and Althaea which is of extraordinary beauty.

The fateful event comes off on Dec; 7th. I have decided to try at St. John's the following week if I fail the first week.

My reading of light literature has practically collapsed and I devour volumes of Freitzchke Socialism, and Greek Art! Incidentally I read 'Unto this Last' in the course of my political studies and was much delighted, especially by the style which is inimitable. I tried to write à la Ruskin in my last essay and degenerated into a barbaric parody of Thompson's Shelley.

I am not yet certain about next holidays as my plans are in a state of chaos. I will write and let you know before long.

With best love

Yours affectionately

C. M. Bowra

Maurice got his scholarship to Oxford, to New College, founded by William of Wykeham. Maurice's last visit to China via Petrograd is fully described in his *Memories*, he also wrote very fully about it to Ella, who looked forward to his letters with delicious impatience. She became interested in things Russian to the extent of buying a Samoyed dog—which Maurice had described as pulling sledges over the snowy Russian steppes, then later he told her about the desirability of owning a white chow, white for Mandarins, and somehow, money being no deterrent, one was found for her, a lovely snowy bitch with an inky tongue. The lawns of the Greenwood were now graced with two large and frolicsome white dogs, both long haired who needed grooming daily; their barks and Ella's tremendous piano work must have made the house busily multisonous. Jimmy, who was getting very old, walked stiffly about the house taking no notice as the two young dogs chased each other up and down the stairs, Henry's longer legs giving him an advantage over Una. The house was constantly full of sound, Ella's singing, the striped awning flapping, or workmen putting in a new floor to the billiard room which was to be her music room.

Suddenly there was panic! Ethel could not find Jimmy. Everyone downed tools to search, pale and tearstained Ethel paced the garden calling and calling. The house was turned upside down . . . no Jimmy. A search party was sent out onto the road, Ethel collapsed in the drawing room, certain that he had been run over. Ella kept her head and called for silence, he might be shut in somewhere. She crept about listening, and was rewarded with the sound of faint barking from under the new billiard room floor. Jimmy was perfectly all right, he had gone to sleep peacefully under the joists and had been floored up. Ethel gave his carpenter rescuer a tip of five pounds, a lot of money in those days.

Busy the house certainly was, but it lacked two things, Men and Children. Ella by now felt that she could survive without a man to lean on, she was capable of running her own and Ethel's affairs, she enjoyed having a big house and garden to organise, she dressed for effect, not to attract, gardened to be praised for her rare plants, not for the love of them, and learnt to play golf to beat, rather than to meet others. She was defiantly cheerful in her loneliness.

It was 1918, there were thousands like her. The slaughter of the 1914–18 war upset marital patterns, the remains of Rupert Brooke's 'half men' had a vast field of eager females to choose from, some of Rupert's lads leapt cleanly into bed leaving a trail of unwanted children. Their swimming had been done in the trenches, who could blame either party, instinct for once was stronger than moral code, soon there were no 'half men' left.

Ella was finding out that money could buy almost everything, it was just a matter of letting the right people know what you wanted, and being patient.

EIGHT

Four Decisive Years

1918 saw Ethel and Ella into the Greenwood and out of their mutual dependence on each other for emotional release and comfort. Always the apparently stronger character, Ella began to spread her wings. Gradually to begin with, after all she was nearing her fortieth birthday, with little worldly experience. First of all there were extravagant dogs to look after, then more trips to London. Much music buying, and experimentation with difficult modern settings of Verlaine by Duparc, and songs by Ravel, Mahler, Strauss, Debussy. Frantically, difficult piano studies by Liszt, all very stimulating and time-consuming, but not enough to use up her enormous energy and assuage her restless temperament. Then with money to burn that autumn, she bought sable furs, custom-made hats and shoes, and acquired a diamond and pearl mini-tiara from the Goldsmiths and Silversmiths. She was developing an image of herself to which she thereafter remained faithful. It did not include a husband. She was never a man hunter, always remaining a little shy and able to blush, opening and closing her hands anxiously when talking to 'nice men'.

Ella was intolerant, though, of men she despised; she bullied male employees, and could best any plumber or decorator who did not carry out her wishes. It was not unusual for men she did not like to be frightened of her.

Ethel was now at the highest peak of her popularity, she had no need for sympathy from Ella although it would have been very welcome. Ella had never liked Ethel's books, still less her short stories, and she was under no obligation now to pretend that she did. Violet Ebsworth could provide the sympathy and understanding of her work, the appreciation of her ideals and her characters which Ethel needed. Violet was soon to become her typist as well as dealer-in-chief with fan mail. A writer's typist must really know the writer intimately, and be able to interpret correctly much over-corrected MSS. It is a labour born of mutual understanding, and ideally, affection; Violet Ebsworth had both attributes.

This situation left Ella without any ties to Ethel except that of love and loyalty. Reggie, who had been contented to let Ella run his life, married unexpectedly and unfortunately; there was little happiness. Ella did not like or approve of her sister-in-law —one wonders if she would really have liked any sister-in-law, however perfect. Unable to organise and push her brother around any more, Ella was at a loose end; there was no more dangerous position for her to be in. Ella's abundant energy could lead her into rash acts.

Having discovered the power of money, she used it to set in motion a series of private investigations which had as their ultimate aim, the tracking down and procuring of an unwanted child of good parentage, with a view to adoption. Ethel fell in with her plans reluctantly, she loved dogs but children were another matter. Ella pointed out that the size of the Greenwood would allow space for a complete nursery wing, it could include accommodation for a nanny and a nursemaid, there would be no need for the child to be either seen or heard by Ethel.

Ella's dark blue restless eyes would have sparkled with excitement, searching over Ethel's face for a look of enthusiasm or pleasure. It was very hard to resist Ella if she wanted her way, and Ethel, loving her as she did, would have found it impossible to reject out of hand anything that would give Ella such great pleasure. She had received very little love in her life, and a child of her own would fill the aching void.

Ethel reluctantly agreed, making one stipulation that Nursie should return, bringing Peggy with her to be the child's companion and part of the household. Ella agreed, saying she had been thinking of that very arrangement herself. She set the necessary machinery in motion and Nursie was informed what was afoot. It was the summer of 1918, the War was nearly over, and Peggy was now three years old, and needed another child to take an interest in. To Nursie the proposition sounded unusual, but possible; in any case she would have done almost anything for Ethel's sake and it was certainly Ethel's doing that she had been offered the job. Apart from this, Ethel was now

famous, her books were to be found in every house, it would be
glamorous to work in the house of such a person. With the war
ending Nursie would have had to look for a job somewhere, so
why not accept?

On the 7th of November 1918, a girl was born, in the none too
salubrious district of Paddington. Her mother had been tabbed
by Ella's spies, and the father was known to her. This baby
fitted Ella's specifications. Negotiations were begun. On the
11th, the Great War ended, a Peace Treaty was signed, England
went mad with joy, the celebrations lasted for two days. On the
25th the child was registered, and named Gladys Olive, the
latter name presumably in recognition of the olive branches
being waved. Olive was two weeks old, puny, a pale baby with
an uncertain future.

Ella alerted Nursie, who arrived at the Greenwood with
Peggy. The house yet again rang with the sound of carpenters
and plumbers, noiseproof doors were installed to separate the
nursery quarters from the rest of the house, new bathrooms
were fitted, day and night nurseries, a separate food lift from
the kitchen, and a bedroom and living room for Nursie and
Peggy.

Gladys Olive, lying in a cradle made of a drawer, had not
seen the sun or breathed fresh air; she had yet to be moved out
of the basement flat where she had been born. At six weeks, her
mother took her to an agreed meeting place in the West End.
It was John Lewis's, the department store in Oxford Street,
which still has the reputation for being 'never knowingly under-
sold'. Here over a cup of coffee, Ella took charge. There did not
appear to be any regrets on the mother's part, at least she did
not show them, probably being far too overawed by Ella's
magnificent presence. If anything else changed hands at the
same time, it has not been recorded.

Ella, bearing Gladys Olive in her arms, swept out of the shop
and into the waiting Daimler, where Nursie was ready to take
charge. To hand were new clothes into which the baby was
thrust, making little complaint. Nursie inspected her and
pronounced. 'Not up to much is she, Miss Ella, we'll have to see
what we can do.' Ella looked and said, 'Olive is a most unsuitable name. It sounds so sallow, I shall call her Poppy.'

I had arrived.

Small babies do not fascinate a woman whose main interest in life is education, so until I could speak it was best to leave me to Nursie.

In the spring of 1919 Ella went off on another trip to France and Switzerland, taking young Patsy Phillips with her. Before they left however, a photograph was taken of Ella holding me, and Ethel holding Jimmy, an 'each unto his own' picture, both seeming very pleased and proud. Ella and Patsy first stayed in a private house on the lakeside, near the town of Annecy, they visited Pont en Royan, and Les Petits Gourlets, Ella entranced at the picturesque poverty of the peasants. Then moving to Chamounix, they stayed in a vast hotel from which they could set out on expeditions to the Glacier des Bossons and the Mer de Glace, climbing and exploring on foot. Patsy paddled in the icy water from the glacier.

Perhaps Ella would have liked Patsy for a sister-in-law, but although this was no longer on the cards, she was determined to show her how much she loved her. They had a wonderful holiday, sharing all the excitements, and in no sense was Patsy considered as a companion. Their friendship blossomed with great mutual affection, they had forged a bond that never broke.

At Guildford I was beginning to put on weight, and become vocal. Ethel who had been left in charge of the household, saw me every day, and taught Jimmy to guard my pram when the big dogs threatened to upset it. Elderly Jimmy kept them well in hand, snapping if they came too close. Nursie and Peggy had their meals with Ethel and were treated exactly like members of the family. When Ella came back from her Swiss tour, this pattern had been established, there was little that she could do about it. Needless to say it had not been her own intention, she had very decided ideas about how to treat employees. Nursie kept quietly smug, Ethel was sweetness itself, Ella was obliged to accept the situation.

With the summer approaching, Ella paid some expensive visits to London, bringing back with her beautiful hand-made clothes for her 'baby'. She never forgot Peggy, who also had a gift every time but of subtly inferior quality which must have been noticed by Nursie. I was beginning to make noises that sounded like names, both sisters listened nervously to hear which of them I would identify first; it was however 'Nana', they both signed with inward relief, Nursie preened and Peggy became jealous.

Ethel, acutely aware of Ella's jealous nature, found herself treading a tightrope, and insisted that Nursie should only take orders from Ella now that she was back again. But as soon as I could walk I undid all her efforts, by staggering towards Ethel, when they both came into the nursery together after a day in London. Ethel's charismatic personality reached out even to a baby, in spite of the fact that she did not really like small children, they made her feel awkward, and she had no idea how to play with them.

That year Ethel wrote *The Altar of Honour*, the story of a girl who escapes the cruel domination of her half-sister, the girl having been born to her father's mistress. Could she have been writing a veiled warning to Ella? What Ethel has experienced so far may have confirmed her opinion that life with Ella had its drawbacks. Ella demanded that her friends and relations should have total devotion to her, if they showed any affection other than towards herself they were liable to be dropped, and possibly sneered at behind their backs. Ethel also feared a rift between herself and Ella, and for me the possibility of a lonely childhood. So she kept herself firmly outside my daily life, thus inhibiting Ella's incipient jealousy, a tragic affliction which ruined many of her friendships. Ella was delightful company, witty, loving, generous, but her conditions of total devotion did not allow her friends to marry or have close friends of their own, activities which she regarded as an affront to herself.

Ella's rich contralto voice resounded over the garden during the summer of 1919, exciting the dogs, waking up the children and vibrating earnestly through the house. It was a hot dry summer, yucca plants flowered for their once-in-twenty-years cycle, the lawns dried up, the dogs gambolled in and out of the open doors, what breeze there was flapped and crackled in the blue striped window shades, the stone bird baths had to be filled daily.

Gustav Mahler was now being favoured, his 'Lied von der Erde', with words translated from the Chinese into German, gave Ella plenty of pleasurable trouble. Her musical sense would never allow her to sing a song in any other language than that of the composer.

In the late summer Maurice Bowra arrived back from China

and immediately came to stay, both sisters thoroughly enjoyed listening to his enthusiastic descriptions of his eastern travels. When it came to discussing Greek philosophy, Ethel would think of something urgent which needed attention in another part of the house.

At the end of this visit, Ella accompanied Maurice to London where they went to a play in the afternoon and on to *Tristan and Isolde* in the evening. Thirty years later Ella remembered the incident as 'a most exhausting day and night'.

Contrary to the myth that Maurice Bowra in his prime rejected those for whom he had no more intellectual use, it is interesting to record that he did, in answer to Ella's congratulations on his knighthood, invite her for a weekend at Wadham College. Ella was by this time in her late seventies, and not in good health.

To her delight his invitation included the use of Vice-Chancellor's chauffeur-driven car there and back. They had two days of reminiscences recounted in the comfort of the Warden's Lodge, encouraged and fortified by good food and drink. This is more than he ever did for his mother who had never been invited to stay with him.

Another visitor at this time from over the road was David Smithers, Sir Waldron Smithers' son, aged eleven, boarding at Boxgrove School. He would be invited to Sunday lunch, a splendid meal which started at eleven o'clock with sherry and Madeira cake (shades of Granny Parrott), then a stroll round the garden admiring dogs, flowers and babies. Followed by much hand scrubbing before a mammoth lunch cooked by Mrs. Coombes from the lodge. Lunch over, Ella would conduct her replete guests to the music room, where she would sing and play to them until tea time. Thin cucumber sandwiches, rich fruit cake, china tea (or lemonade if preferred), all set in a drawing room full of heavy comfort and the smell of greenhouse flowers massed in Georgian winecoolers.

All guests were treated equally, the young and the old, the learned and the simple, it was a stimulating atmosphere for a small boy to experience, rubbing shoulders with adults on equal terms. A principle of Ella's which Ethel bowed to rather than agreed with. She thought children had their right place and shouldn't interrupt grown-ups. In spite of the presence of

Nursie, Peggy and myself at all meals, a habit which she herself had insisted on, Ethel did not bring small children into her books at this time. Her narrative dealt mostly with pre-nuptial courtship, leaving the reader firmly at the bedroom door, a feature she considered to be the reason for her success. Children are mentioned as a necessary ingredient to a story, but are seldom described convincingly, she found it difficult to be interested in youth unless pubescence had been reached and could be taken into consideration. Ella, however, really loved the young, and regretted their having to mature into adults. Maurice Bowra was her ideal, he had no permanent attachments, no wife to be jealous of, he was the eternal student with a scintillating mind, and above all was caustically witty. His brilliance both fascinated and awed her. Maurice's appearance at the Greenwood that summer was to be his last before going to Oxford, where he was to spend the rest of his life. He would have been the last to have expected such a future, but Ella was never surprised at his eventual rise to Vice-Chancellorship and knighthood. 'He always had it in him,' she would say, 'and knew how to use his brain.'

David Smithers also knew how to use his brain, and although Ella did not have so much to do with the moulding of his intellectual powers, her attitude towards him must have had its effect, she was an expert listener, and never tried to lead the conversation. She must have cared considerably for the future of Waldron's son, an innocent and indirect link with old times best forgotten—somehow they never were. How curious it is that one of the last trips that Professor Sir David Smithers has taken is to China by invitation of the Government of the Chinese Republic leading a medical delegation researching acupuncture. When Sir David visited the Great Wall, did he hear Maurice's youthful footsteps behind him? Or see his ghost?

Mention has been made of Mrs. Coombes as an expert cook. Her husband was an equally accomplished gardener, and it was he who organised the flowers and their rotation, with never a gap to be found, never a leaf out of line or a break in the serried ranks of colour. Ella waged a continual war against this regimentation which Coombes found totally incomprehensible. He had been a public gardens gardener all his life; if it wasn't neat circles then it must be straight lines, and no messing about with clumps of this and that. He thought Ella a very queer fish, and was quite capable of going out at night with a lamp to straighten out any softening of the lines that Ella had ordered. Coombes loved the dogs, and they him, and when it was supper time Ella used to stand on the terrace and call in her best contralto singing voice . . . 'Henreaah, Unaah'. If they did not come at once she would say crossly, 'Coombes again, I expect' and walk off towards the bottom of the garden where sure enough she would find the two dogs happily sitting in Coombes's wheelbarrow having a ride, a pleasure they could never resist. Coombes would smile slowly, as if to say 'Serves you right for messing up my garden yesterday'.

Ethel did not notice growing flowers, her eyes were focused at a higher level. Trees, creepers, flowering shrubs, hiding places for the watching lover, arbours, garden seats, even greenhouses were secret meeting places and of much more interest to her than blossoms in a flower bed. Birdsong indicated either the arrival of a loved one, or the means of communicating with one. She endowed birds with human thoughts, to be expressed at the appointed moment in suitably modulated tones. Her ornithological acumen was extremely limited. Avian rarities neither appear, nor are mentioned by any of her characters. Blackbirds and thrushes were sometimes transposed into mavis and throstle, to avoid repetition, still birds even by another name. . . .

By the end of 1919 two more of Ethel's books were published. *The Lamp in the Desert* and *The Tidal Wave*.

Then Reggie unexpectedly announced the birth of his first son, Don. They soon came to stay, all other visitors were put off for the duration of the visit. Nursie was shocked and Ella distressed by their behaviour. Ella offered to adopt Don. She found herself on the receiving end of a stream of invective from her sister-in-law, and for the first time in her life did not draw herself up and stalk away. Ella genuinely wanted to help a child in trouble. So she kept her temper, and Reggie's everlasting affection, strengthened over the years by the generosity of both sisters. Don did not survive long, as prophesied by Nursie.

NINE

The Obstacle Race

THE NEW year—1920—did not begin auspiciously. Jimmy now thirteen years old, developed cancer and the vet advised putting him to sleep. Ethel was horrified, to take his life seemed wicked after all that he had done for her. She shut herself up with Jimmy in her bedroom. Ella knew that it would be the kindest way out, so she positioned herself outside Ethel's door, and started gently to persuade.

'Nettie darling, are you listening?' A tearful 'yes'.

'Nettie, it would be kindest you know.'

'Sissie darling, how could it be kindest to kill?'

And so the gentle coaxing went on until Ethel reluctantly gave way and Jimmy was put to sleep while she held his paw, and talked to him through her tears. She had insisted that the drug should be administered so that he should not know when he was having a final shot. Ethel kept the vet there nearly all day, the entire household was disrupted and in a state of mourning. Ella ordered Coombes to take the big dogs for a long walk, then shut them up in the greenhouse. Nursie was to keep Peggy and me in the nursery. While Ethel was occupied with Jimmy and the vet, she took the garden boy and chose a suitable spot for Jimmy's grave. It was to be dug very deep.

When it was all over, an exhausted Ethel carried Jimmy wrapped in his own blanket, to the graveside. Ella put his old basket at the bottom, he was laid in it as if curled up alseep, his favourite ball beside him. Another blanket was laid over his body and the grave filled in. For several weeks Ethel genuinely mourned, he had been her constant companion day and night. Missing him appallingly, she slept badly and ate even less than ever. Fortunately the book *The Princesses' Game* was finished and due to be published in the spring.

It was her habit to have a rest and change when her books came out, thus avoiding the press. Ella persuaded her with difficulty to take a few days off. They were driven in Martha to the Lake District. Staying at Windermere they met a Miss Edith de Wolf, having a short holiday away from her ancient mother. Ella liked Edith, but Ethel found her too ugly to be attractive, though redeemed by the small wirehaired terrier she had with her. Ethel was full of advice, glad to be talking small-dog shop with someone so sympathetic. He was a young dog and Edith really had no idea how to train him at all. Some of the sadness of Jimmy's demise wore off as they all three went for long walks, in perfect weather. They found wild daffodils, and came back to their hotel bedrooms with hands full of violets and primroses. Ella began to be fascinated with Edith, who really had little to attract her except her love of music, and a willingness to be pushed around. Edith thought Ella quite glamorous, with her exotic dress sense and daring independence and began to have what can only be described as a schoolgirl crush, much to Ella's amusement. When the holiday was over, addresses were exchanged, Ella promising to invite Edith to stay. Not until her first visit, did Edith realise who Ethel was, a fine triumph for Ella to be wanted for her own sake.

In June Mary Bastard came to stay, an old friend from their school days at the Shrubbery. Mary was yet another spinster with an old mother to look after. Since the War they had gone to live at Lancing, where Mrs. Bastard kept Pekinese dogs and Marmalade cats. Her family had been amongst the first to cross Africa from the Cape to Kenya, travelling by bullock cart. Being of such extremely tough stock, she would brook no softness on the part of her very pretty daughter, whose personality was of the gentlest. Mary did not have a chance to be herself, and although she had many young men interested and in love with her, none was strong enough to bear the burden of old Mrs. Bastard as a mother-in-law. Mary came to Guildford as a respite from home duties while her brother Segar was home on leave. I was eighteen months old by then; she was delighted with me, and thoroughly enjoyed playing with me in the garden. Having no prospect of shedding her own motherly burden, she envied Ella her good fortune and independence. Also, and with reason, since Ethel's book were a great solace to her, she adored Ethel and enjoyed Ella, a situation which Ella sought to reverse over the years.

By midsummer it was time for Ethel to have the proper holiday which she had forgone in the spring. She reluctantly agreed
to share a holiday with Ella, Nursie, and the children in the Isle
of Wight. They stayed at a hotel in Shanklin, close to the sea
and shingle. The weather was brilliant, Peggy jumped about in
the waves, draped in a long-legged bathing dress, her red-gold
curls dancing in the sun. I was introduced to paddling and sand-
castles.

Ethel began to relax and enjoy herself, the setting pleased her,
although she gave Ella some anxious moments, by insisting on
wandering about on the cliffs alone after dinner. In *The Obstacle
Race* which she was at the time planning, and dedicated to Mary
Bastard, there is an excellent description of such a walk, and
the dog Columbus was surely her way of perpetuating the
memory of her beloved Jimmy. Ella also remembered those
nightingales, but in a copse much further inland. The heroine
of this book bears a striking resemblance to Ethel, both physical
and mental, a dual personality set in a very ladylike frame.
There is mention of a small child being brought in with the
gingerbread pudding to be shown off. Mrs. Coombes had grand-
children, and the long gossipy description by 'Juliet's' landlady,
on the subject of local people could well have been taken from
her conversations with Ethel who always listened delightedly
to her outpourings—a failing which brought disapproval from
Nursie and annoyance from Ella, for wasting cook's time.

There are no pictures of Ethel at this time, but one of Ella and
me on the Shanklin hotel lawns reveals her elegance, so tall and
slim with her beautifully pleated white summer dress reaching
to her ankles. It must have been about now that my first memories of Ella begin, of being held up to a window to see a rainbow, of large hands holding me too tightly, a big nose close to
my face, a prickly brooch sticking into my arm. I was most
unhappy and quite unable to see the rainbow through my tears.
Then Nursie took me and said firmly, 'Be-ave yourself, Poppy'.
It was her war cry, without it I should have been impossibly
spoilt.

After her return from the Isle of Wight, Ethel received a
letter from A. S. Watt, who now handled all her literary work,
telling her that he had sold dramatic rights in *The Knave of
Diamonds*. Ethel was very pleased, but refused to attend any

meeting with the management or the directors, saying she would willingly talk to the actors and actresses, but in her own home and one at a time.

Violet Vanbrugh had been chosen as leading lady, although she was really much too serious an actress for the part, but times were difficult, and she accepted. Ethel was touchingly humble, and asked her if she would care to spend a few days at the Greenwood to discuss her part. Violet accepted, asking if she could bring her sister Irene with her. Preparations began in Guildford.

Violet Ebsworth was asked to come over and take shorthand, and tactfully to help to entertain the guests. Ella practised her most difficult piano works, probably Liszt's Transcendental Studies after Paganini, her favourite 'showing off' piece, determined that the Vanbrugh Sisters should realise that the Dell sisters were as cultured as they were rich. Coombes went over his flower beds with a tooth comb and ruler, Mrs. Coombes made vol-au-vent pastry cases, the larder dripped with pheasant and hare, Nursie washed her charges' hair and starched their best frocks, red shoes were bought now that I also could use them. Ella arranged and re-arranged tiers of greenhouse flowers in the drawing room. The chauffeur was sent to fetch them in a sparkling Martha.

The fact that actresses enjoy being recognised had not registered with Ethel and Ella, and there was no crowd of enthusiasts to wave to them as they entered the drive. Violet and Irene looked at the empty gateway and said in the same breath, 'How extraordinary!' The chauffeur, thinking that they had spoken to him, asked, 'Is everything all right, Madam?' so Violet asked him if he had forgotten to tell the Press. His reply 'Oh no, Madam, I wouldn't have dreamed of it', gave them a suspicion of the sort of weekend they were in for.

Readers of Ethel's books usually imagined that she was feminine, fluffy, and affected. Violet and Irene may well have had this image in their minds as they drove up to the front door. This tall pale-faced, tragic-eyed woman was not what they were expecting nor for that matter were the rest of the family. There were no family men, not even absent men to talk about. There was not much drink, a sherry before lunch and an abstemious glass of wine with dinner. Yet these women and children were happy, they radiated enjoyment. The Vanbrugh sisters had never seen anything quite like it, and were intrigued. Violet must have understood very quickly why Lady Carfax, whose role she played, was so entirely pure in the face of temptation. Ethel's temptations were imagined, and there was a limit even to that—the point where her heroine said 'No'. Though neither sister had much experience of real men, Ella was more down to earth and approachable. Violet made a point of making friends with her, and they even laughed kindly together at Ethel's romanticism. Violet Vanbrugh explained her need of publicity at that time, saying Ethel's great popularity would be a help. She was, however, at pains to make sure that Ella understood she did not find her part at all congenial; it was for her a slightly ridiculous role to have to play. Ella did not, of course, tell Ethel then, but when the play was put on she soon became aware of it.

TEN

Ideally Wicked

ACTIVE WRITERS, and novelists in particular, have little
time for close and constant friends, how can they? There is no
time to spare from the friends created in their books. A writer's
life is lonely—but by choice, his own originations being his first
loves. Real people are the source material from which the
novelist creates his characters. To make your own mixture of
personal qualities, then clothe it in human flesh of your own
choosing—what a Godlike activity, and who does not like
playing God?

How tiresome, then, the ready-made article seems, time has
to be spent finding out how and why he ticks. Create a person
and the clockwork is your own invention, perfectly understood
and tailormade for the part he has to play. All perfectionists
suffer, particularly those who are creative, the imperfect God-
made human is so faulty and tiresome. Take a good story,
people it with ideal characters to fit—what have you? Theoretic-
ally the perfectly balanced tale. What if the actors are too perfect
for their parts, where is the edge if the story is peopled by prigs
and demons, but seldom the faulty humans one meets in real
life? You have a splendid tale spoilt by its inhuman players.

This fault could not happen to a writer who had got out into
the world and *suffered* other people of all kinds in order to be
able to write about them convincingly.

Ethel observed humanity distantly, her shyness and reserved
manners forbidding any real intimacy outside her immediate
family. Most of her characters are drawn from this source, but
also from her cooks and parlourmaids. Where Ella made close
and rewarding friends, Ethel cashed in on the side, obtaining
devotion and love in an oblique way through the medium of her
writing, though very seldom in a personal way, since Ella
fenced her in. Ethel was not above including Ella's friends in her

books, all suitably disguised to avoid detection. Ethel's feet
may seldom have touched solid earth for long, but her charm lay
in being elusive yet delightful when cornered.

She has always been heavily criticised for her slipshod,
mushy writing, for her continual repetitions of commonplace
words. Yet her books are well planned, the plots are good, the
story unfolds enticingly. What happens next is always of paramount importance, the reader is unable to put the book down.
Her great fault lies in over-dramatisation. It is difficult to read
some of the passages now (they were written with almost holy
sincerity) without laughing aloud.

> A great shaft of red sunlight burst suddenly through the
> heaped storm clouds in the west. He turned and faced it,
> dazzled but strangely exultant. He felt as if his whole being
> had been plunged into a glowing flame. The wonder of it
> pulsed through him. As it were involuntarily, a prayer sprang
> to his lips. 'Oh God, make me more worthy.' Then he turned
> as if the glory had become too much for him, and went into
> the house. (*The Obstacle Race*).

Yet what a satisfying passage to have written providing you
have experienced such a thing in your mind. Ethel also preached
her own brand of Gospel in *The Obstacle Race*, as throughout her
works.

> 'Do you think you can defy me?' fumed Fielding. 'I am sure
> of it,' said Dick. 'I can defy the whole world if I choose.
> There is a certain portion of man that can't be beat if he plays
> fair, however hard he's hammered. It's the rule of the game.'

Ethel was also a woman of her time and to her these were
current and acceptable sentiments.

How she hates the 'goodlooking beast' and hastily puts a
sneer across his face lest her reader be led astray. In a very
masochistic way she also makes her heroes wait for satisfaction.
In a passage from *The Obstacle Race*, the hero and heroine have
been necking seriously, and both enjoying it, but when they
pause to draw breath she makes the girl say, 'Not again, please
not again', then a few seconds after that, 'I want you to be just
friends with me again'. The Hero, 'In public you mean?'

Heroine, 'No in private too'. She then later remarks that the girl 'was superbly happy provided that it didn't go any further'. Here one senses Ethel's own desire to be left inviolate, she was fearful of reality through ignorance, caused by her instinctive personal withdrawl from any physical ties. Yet her curiosity and longing must have been acute, why else should she have spent her life writing about love and passion, to which she was a comparative stranger?

Edward Shanks, writing in 1922, compared her with D. H. Lawrence, saying that he could write but that his stories were not good, and that Ethel could not write but that her stories were good. Shanks also accused her of vulgarity, which then meant lack of taste, rather than crudity, as now. Certainly her written obsession with 'high breeding' and verbal class distinctions seems dated and tasteless, 'That subtle something— a distinction of bearing' or 'She rose and came forward, tall and graceful, bearing the unmistakable stamp of high breeding in every delicate movement'. In 1920 this would not have been taken amiss by domestics as it was the essence of glamour to be in the service of 'well born' people, but one wonders how the 'well born' people themselves liked it.

Ethel does come near to being shockingly vulgar when she describes, not once but several times, a hunched back boy as being like a baboon, yet her aim was to engender pity not disgust. As a writer repetition was her great undoing, she plunged on, interested in the unfolding of the drama rather than in how she was telling it. She sensed no need for a fresh way of describing an emotion, her books abound in bodies and faces that 'quiver, shudder, tremble, pulse, flutter and throb'. Absurd things happen, especially to the eyes, which 'sink, jump, pierce, search, flame, flash and smoulder,' then turn to 'onyx or ice'. One poor man is wall-eyed, and this proves to be a serious barrier to understanding his inner being.

There are maddeningly 'soft' incidents, father and son (adult) hold hands, a heroine 'kisses her dog between the eyes', a full colonel says 'pooh!' when sympathising with his son. Boats thrill with movement, women are apt to kneel at open windows preferably at night—arms flung wide pleading with fate, while birds understand, and dogs smile.

In what may have been a deliberate attempt to understand

her conflicting emotions, as part of her re-thinking of her own
way of life, Ethel has drawn up a comparable double-sided
character in 'Rosa Mundi', whose name is also the title of the
short story in which she appears. A much talked of and admired
dancer, well-known as a demi-mondaine with many lovers, is
also a pure innocent childlike half-woman, and assumes these
conflicting roles according to the demands of the situation. The
dancer's 'hero' is a man whose piety makes him reject her. By
the time he discovers that she has another side to her character
he is too late to rescue her from the vulgar marriage to a
promoter which she is undertaking to make an honest woman of
herself. Here there is the dual personality set in an *unladylike*
frame.

Rosa Mundi is one of a collection of short stories published in
1921. They are less mature than her book *The Obstacle Race*.
Perhaps her publisher realised that she was at a peak of popularity, and that almost anything from her hand would be un-
critically read. They may even have been early rejected work.

Each story has really good bone structure, yet the word-flesh
is flabby. It hangs untidily, garnished with such tawdry sym-
bolism that it takes a considerable effort to read it. Inasmuch as
we all find difficulty in finding ourselves, Ethel had also placed
herself in a vacuum of voluntary solitary confinement, and with
this in mind it is interesting to read her views on friendship.
'The best definition of a friend is one who will help in time of
trouble' (*Sown Amongst Thorns*); there is no suggestion of
enjoying a friend's company. On marriage 'Marriage is such a
mix-up of soul and body, and I think I should be rather afraid
that the body might win, and the other part, the spiritual part,
get crowded out' (*Serpent in The Garden*). Ethel was frightened
of her latent sexuality and masochistic tendencies; with reason,
for her descriptions of whippings are intimate, frequent, and
told with relish. She obviously liked violence, it gave her a
frisson, as in the following passages from *The Knave of Diamonds*,
where a man is 'thrashed' to within an inch of his life.

> Once she heard a curse, and once a demoniacal laugh, and
> once thrilling her through and through . . . a dreadful sound
> that was like the cry of a stricken animal . . . and still that
> awful flail-like sound went on until all sound of voices

ceased . . . Nap . . . was hanging like a wet rag from the
merciless grip that upheld him, and though his limp body
seemed to shudder at every crashing blow, he made no
voluntary movement of any sort . . . She knelt beside the
huddled unconscious figure and tried to straighten out the
crumpled limbs. The sweater had been torn from his back,
and the shirt beneath was in bloodstained tatters. His face
was covered in blood, . . . great purple welts crossed and re-
crossed each other on the livid features. The bleeding lips
were drawn back in a devilish grimace.

It is interesting to note that this unfortunate man was only a
good friend at the time, having been mistaken for a lover, and
this was his reward for helping in time of trouble. Ethel does
not confine her casualties to men, in the same book the unfortunate heroine has to conceal her neck in a scarf to hide the
red weal raised by her husbands' riding whip. A similar beating
takes place in *The Prey of the Dragon*, a story with the moral that,
however bad a man may be, he can be saved by the love of a
good woman. Love, goodness, belief in God, will bring happiness and the key to heaven, no matter what cruelties and passions
have to be borne.

Ethel's women definitely bore their passions, there was little
hint of reciprocal fire. However weak her flesh, woman was
expected to bear up bravely through horrors, illness, rough
handling, and shock, her endurance culminating in a fainting
fit if there was no other way out. All in all, she made quite a
collection of different ways to pass out.

Prayers for guidance abound: 'Oh my God show me the way,
please show me the way' from *Sown Amongst Thorns*. Religious
images flash on and off so frequently that the reader ceases to be
surprised and annoyed that each act cannot be immediately
traced to its source. Washing of feet, washing of hands, people
are lost and found, and even die and are raised up again, as in
the last sentence of *Sown Amongst the Thorns*, putting the
heroine on equal terms with Jesus.

Two women talking about a male casual acquaintance . . . 'I
always feel as if I want to confess my sins to him.' Later when
the man in question comes in (Blake Grange, V.C.), he modestly
depreciates himself after being called a lion with 'Only an Ass

in a Lionskin, my dear Daisy'. Nick, the true hero, in a burst of
helpful advice tells Will to pray:

> 'It isn't just praying now and then that does it, you've got
> to keep up the steam, never slack for an instant, whatever
> happens . . . If you've only got the grit to go on praying hard
> even against your own convictions, you'll get it sooner or
> later . . . They say God doesn't always grant prayer because
> the thing you want may not do you any good. That's gammon,
> futile gammon . . . It's sheer pluck that counts. Nothing else,
> the pluck to go on fighting when you know perfectly well
> you're beaten, the pluck to hang on and worry, worry, worry
> till you get your heart's desire, I'm doing it myself, and God
> knows I shan't give him any peace until I'm satisfied.'

All this from her best seller and *first* novel *The Way of an
Eagle*. It is a revelation of the era in which she wrote. Such
sentiments were the moral backbone of the late Victorians, and
may well have precipitated the selfless slaughterings that were
perpetrated in the name of duty, God and bravery, during the
First World War; each side was crusading for the Glory of God
and England, or God and Germany, neither side believed that
with God's backing they could fail to win.

Ethel missed out badly on convincing descriptions of the
countryside, towns and clothes. Rather than take a good look at
a dusty gritty road, she only feels it under foot and breathes the
dust, and of towns there is only a faint hum of distant traffic with
a few twinkling lights dimly seen. Clothes are gripped and
torn, or just put on, there is no interest in materials, which for
a woman writer is unusual. There is attempted interest in *Rosa
Mundi*, where the gold lamé dress embellished with gold roses
heaped upon the breast sounds prickly and uncomfortable, but
not wickedly enticing as she meant it to be.

Hats have a very sinister fascination; large brimmed and
dark, they hide either tearstained or over made-up faces. Hats
are also donned at both supper and breakfast when confidence
needs boosting. Ethel herself always wore hats out of doors,
even when taking the dog for a walk; they gave her a feeling of
protection from curious eyes.

One wonders why she wrote at all when writing was obviously not her medium, nor was she prepared to better it with

Ethel at Ashford, 1912, on the day when *The Way of an Eagle* was published

With Ella and Maurice Bowra, 1919

Ethel (aged 34)
and Ella (aged 36),
Christmas 1915

Engaged – Ethel and
Gerald, 1922

1. March 1937

My own darling Elizabeth.
Here is my new
book with my very
best love. It came
out last Thursday.
I do hope you will
like it, darling.
How are you? Not
snowed up, I hope!
Have you heard any
more about Uncle Will?
I mustn't stay for
more now, as I have

several other parcels
to send off.
My very best love,
darling.
Always your own most
loving Nellie

A letter from Ethel to Ella,
March 1937

Violet Ebsworth, Ethel's much-loved friend and secretary

Photo: Valentine

Ethel and Ella at St Mary's, Winchester

polishing. Could she have been a doer rather than a thinker? Religious activities spring to mind, a married female priest, a Bishop's wife? Certainly people who remember her at this time say that she reminded them of a vicar's wife. Yet she was too sexually aware, a totally innocent yet adult nymphet laced up into a binding moral code. How could she have advised and guided people in distress? All her heroines and their lovers play advance and retreat games, blowing now hot, now cold. Does she not do this herself in the very telling, longing for fulfilment, yet holding back in case—in case of what? Total commitment is for ever, she had to be so sure.

Using her writing as an escape valve was a pleasant way of expressing herself, it was also morally satisfactory; that she was most avidly read was a welcome financial bonus which did her no harm as long as Ella happily spent it. Good was definitely being done, she need have no qualms on account of her wealth.

Dialogue is perhaps Ethel's greatest achievement. It is simple and reproduces exactly how ordinary people would have talked at that time. In its ordinariness, it may be disappointing, and unless the speaker can convey his status by conversational quirks, Ethel does not attempt to lift what he says out of a humdrum hit and return game. The speech she gives her characters may be banal, but most of it is entirely credible.

Where then lies the magic, is this very odd mixture of ideal cum wicked people talking in a very commonplace way the key to her enormous success, is it possible to identify more closely if what is said is totally understandable? Can the trip be taken so much more easily?

Her religious aspirations? These are something to be taken into more serious consideration. Ethel was a good and spiritual person, leading the life she preached, by instinctive choice. Virginity was imperative before marriage (for women!) and an unswerving belief in God and his goodness. Moral fibres were not just tough, they were threads of steel. Others came before oneself, duty was paramount and performed with a cheerful smile, blackguards were vanquished, but not without a helping hand in trouble. True love was a sacred thing not to be turned into sin.

ELEVEN

Theatricals

THERE was however one facet of the life the two sisters were leading which was less seraphic, and demanded facing up to. Ella was presumably going to go through with my adoption, there was no indication from my mother that she wanted to have me back. What Ella may have begun as a sentimental experiment, was now a factual problem to be resolved. She was certainly emotionally involved, yet beginning to realise that the life of an unmarried mother who openly and delightedly showed off her baby, was not, as now, fashionable or acceptable. Ella was ahead of her times, she remembered her mother's warning too late.

People scandal-mongered, especially those who knew her only as Ethel M. Dell's sister. Had she slipped up? Who was my father? Why didn't she get married, with all that money surely it was no problem? Why did the Dell household seethe with unmarried women? There was also a fascinating rumour of a brother and his drunken wife, who brawled and ill-treated their baby.

Temporary parlour maids were waylaid by the Press, and remuneratively questioned. Nursie also came in for a raised eyebrow, another fatherless child? What was a well-known authoress doing? Running a home for needy ladies? And if necessary their babies? A short story was published in one of the leading newspapers, no names and no towns were mentioned, but the content was aimed at the pious Ethel. Ella was shown it and was outraged, and through solicitors tried to bring the publishers to court, bravely revealing herself as the true target of the article. She was advised to drop the idea as there was nothing to bring them to court for, unnamed insinuation is not actionable. Money was of no avail here, and the damage had been done.

How much this influenced their future is not certain, but

change was in the air, new friends were soon to come into their
lives. Ella meanwhile surrounded herself with her old and
trusted companions. It was nearly Christmas 1920, and they
planned to have a proper festivity, since both children were old
enough now to enjoy the fun.

Maurice and Edward Bowra were invited for the week, and
accepted. Mr. Haddock, Ethel's accountant whom she shared
with Rudyard Kipling and who was a member of the firm of A. P.
Watt, her agents, agreed shyly to put in an appearance, he was
in the same age group as Cyril Ebsworth who came with his
sister Violet. Patsey Philips and Evelyn Vidler were invited to
entertain the Bowras, and a new friend Norah Savage accepted
happily. 'The Cassan' who had introduced the Savages to the
Dells could not be spared from her mother's bedside, neither
could Mary Bastard or Edith de Wolf, so it was to be a much
better balanced group of people than before.

Ella's new friend Norah Savage was built of much the same
material as herself, and although not so tall she had the same
determination, an aptitude for sweeping aside those who did not
march with her. All went well between them provided that they
progressed in the same direction. Norah, who had more worldly
acumen than Ella, tried to smooth out any path that they trod
together. Norah had plans, and coming from a military family
she directed her campaign with careful strategy. Going for long
walks with Ella and the dogs, Norah described her military
brother Gerald in the greatest detail. This, 'quiet, self-effacing,
brave man' would soon be on leave. Ella was, as she was
intended to be, intrigued and told Ethel all about him. They
decided that on no account should he be left out of any of the
festivities.

Perhaps for the first time in her life Ethel realised that there
was an aura of glamour about her that she could exploit to
advantage, she treated herself to a large and beautiful grey
Daimler, which she christened Lady Jane Grey, who arrived in
time for the Christmas holiday, to be profaned, as Edward
Bowra put it, by being used for holly gathering. The two young
men, trampling on her roof to reach out of the way branches
noticed that Gerald Savage was in evidence, and interested in
Ethel.

Ethel must have put aside her writing for that week, and

joined in the preparations. Doing so would have given her time
to watch this Gerald of whom she had heard so much, this
paragon who could surely not exist outside her own books.
Perhaps Gerald hastily read *The Way of an Eagle*, and struggled
metaphorically into Nick Ratcliffe's skin, in preparation for
meeting Ethel. Whatever the reasons, mutual interest was
established.

Christmas presents were generous that year, Ella gave Ethel
a large Della Robbia wall plaque, and received in exchange a
gold mounted shagreen dressing table set, which fitted into a
crocodile carrying case. The children had brooches from
London, Peggy's gold and pearls, and mine gold, pearls and
diamonds, a chicken peering at a pearl egg on a long bar.
Money seemed to be common, even Mary Bastard living with
her widowed mother in what Ella described as penury, managed
to buy the collected works of Rupert Brooke for Ella, putting
inside it a sentimental card about passionate friendship. For
Ethel she had bought James Elroy Flecker, also a collected
edition. In touching gratitude Ethel dedicated her book *The
Obstacle Race* to Mary and called her 'Her dear Half Sister' which
must have annoyed Ella.

The two younger women certainly made the party a success,
Patsy was to see something of Maurice and Edward in the
future, although she was slow to make up her mind. Like Ethel
she enjoyed her freedom. Such a pretty, charming and lively girl,
she had many admirers yet remained shy and retiring for very
many years. Evelyn Vidler was a good sort, jolly, well-covered,
and full of fun, a very stable character with no flights of fancy,
whom it would have been difficult to take for a ride.

Ella had Cyril Ebsworth to keep her company, Violet Ebsworth had to be satisfied with Mr. Haddock, who it turned out
was also an Edward Lear fan, they could be heard reciting 'And
who so happy,—oh who, as the duck and the kangaroo' as they
struggled into coats and galoshes for a post-prandial skip
around the garden.

The year that had begun in such a sad way, now ended on a
flourish of excitement and anticipation. Ethel's first play was
about to be put on, and she had an admirer whom she did not
despise. Ella seemed to be as happy and contented as could be
expected for anyone so demanding of life.

Nurse Talbot, yet Nursie to all, must have found her position tricky. She was an employee, yet treated as one of the family, having all her meals with Ella and Ethel, which would have included dinner in the evening, giving her a welcome opportunity to get out of her uniform, and sit in the drawing room afterwards, sewing and talking. Every night Ethel would still slink off to an early bed, that she might rise at four o'clock to work. Nursie never managed to like Ella, and found her arrogance intolerable, never feeling at ease with her as she did with Ethel. Those evenings meant for relaxation must have been a great ordeal, brought up as she had been on a farm in Devon in the midst of a large and noisy family. Nursie could find no interest in Ella's music nor sympathy for her tendency either to brood or to show off. Being a most honest and straightforward person it would have been impossible for Nursie to simulate any interest, and worse she could not hide her worship of Ethel. Ella strangely enough admired Nursie very much and would dearly have liked her feeling to have been reciprocated; her firm treatment of the children won genuine admiration, particularly her strict attention to total impartiality between Peggy and myself. I could almost have been Nursie's own, so careful was she that I was not favoured, and most certainly she mothered me whereas Ella only occasionally played with me until I could verbally make my wishes known.

Spring 1921 brought the publication of *The Obstacle Race* and *Rosa Mundi*, the last including, besides the title story, a number of tales, some based on topical subjects such as the Amritsar Riots of 1919 when Anglo-Indian feeling was running high, and on the forming of the First Kenya Rifles, soon after General Smuts took Dar es Salaam, removing the Germans from East Africa. These tales are fictional rather than historical, and may well have been researched in the *Illustrated London News*, another source of Ethel's for information.

Edward Thompson writing in *The Other Side of the Medal* (1925), says 'The tensions existing in India has been bad for our race, and a conception of Indian life based upon the writings of Ethel M. Dell and Maud Oliver and even Kipling, has not helped.' Ethel had oversimplified theories, those that were *for* us, were brave, good, selfless, loyal; those against were wicked, traitorous, filthy, and cruel. Basic reasons for their individual needs to fight and win were never analysed, Ethel was not a political animal, her emotions were too near the surface; swayed by human physical feelings rather than human consideration and thought, she did not contemplate the longterm result. Her writing is immediate, almost journalistic, the reader is on the spot all the time, there is no time to stop and think.

There was plenty of real time for pondering, however, about her new friend Lieut. Col. Gerald Tahourdin Savage, D.S.O. He was based on Hertford, once his leave was over, and a correspondence commenced. Ethel's Indian inaccuracies became minimal. Ella found her much more interested in what the postman brought, and a nameless fear quickened her heartbeats as she watched Ethel eagerly sifting the letters. Could it be conceivable that Ethel was in love? At her age, and with all her emotions so ably taken care of by Ella? Surely not! Ethel was to be forty that August, it was ridiculous. Ella put aside the horrid thought and concentrated on her baby, going out of her way to make friends with younger women who had children so that Peggy and I could be asked to parties, which that summer seemed to favour fancy dress. It gave Ella an opportunity to invent some highly original costumes which she made most beautifully by hand, thoroughly enjoying the chance to express her artistry.

Irene and Violet Vanbrugh spent a weekend in March staying at Greenwood, probably to imbibe Ethel's unique and unusual atmosphere, a mixture which Violet had to conjure up on stage. Ella suspected that Violet, used as she was to Shakespearean parts, would have enjoyed playing Lady Carfax more had the role shown less bathos and more humour. Ethel's language and plot must have been difficult for her to interpret in the approved 'Dell manner'. If Ethel had been blessed with a little more sense of the absurd, she would have been so much happier and so much less rich.

The *Knave of Diamonds* opened at the Globe Theatre on 23rd April, 1921. The audience broke the sixpenny seals on their programmes, read the cast in order of appearance, glanced at the synopsis of scenery, and then directed their glance to the bottom of the page where a sticker had been placed over the extracts of rules of the Lord Chamberlain, reading thus:

April 23rd. *Knave of Diamonds.* Globe.
The Knave of Diamonds is as wildly improbable as some of the
true tales told us by certain acquaintances when their
imaginations are set working by fermented inspiration. The
play is adapted from a story by Ethel M. Dell, so it is futile
to dispraise it by saying that it is Dellish. If we do not welcome her material, we welcome Violet Vanbrugh back to
London. There was a time when the Vanbrugh Sisters had
been ousted by the Dolly Sisters.

No source was given for this comment and it is difficult to
understand why the management elected to quote it. They need,
however, have had no doubts about the play's reception. 'The
audience of Saturday seemed thoroughly to enjoy this caricature
of society manners, and applauded before, during and after
every act' (*The Times*, April 25th). That was the audience
though, who seldom go to the theatre to pick holes; they are
prepared to be entertained and titillated, and in this case by their
favourite authoress.

Ethel was an easy target for the critics. There was no need to
search for the weak line, poor plot, or stilted dialogue; they
were all there in abundance. The same issue of *The Times*
quoted above ran an eleven-inch review of the play, headed
'Miss Violet Vanbrugh's Return'. The detailed description of
the play's action includes the remark: 'It is not a very distinguished play, but that may not prevent it from being a good
"filler".' After this evident swipe at the class of audience likely
to go to it, *The Times*'s dramatic critic continues: '. . . It is
nothing more than a very genteel melodrama. It deals with the
human passions and emotions in a thoroughly genteel way and
the authoress (or adaptor) occasionally seems to be rather
terrified by the desperate situations into which some of the
puppets have worked themselves.'

There is also a complaint that the wife-beating husband who
appears in the first act (in hunting pink), does not return. Had
Ethel allowed herself to be consulted, she would no doubt have
enjoyed making him perform yet again, she was at one with her
audience on this point. And it is only fair to point out that the
gentility of speech may have been the fault of the adaptor, the
book having been written some ten years previously, before the

Great War, when ordinary speech was much more stilted than it had become by 1921.

Arkay, in *The Tatler* of May 11th, devotes an entire page to the *Knave of Diamonds*, ripping it apart this time in a most genteel manner himself. 'And now Miss Violet Vanbrugh gives us a dramatised version of Miss Ethel M. Dell's popular story . . . and it is an entirely unadulterated "housemaid's classic" such as we all loved years ago.' What an admission! Continuing with a sarcastic description of the plot and also calling the characters puppets '. . . she . . . received a deservedly tremendous reception . . . played a totally unsuitable part with a cleverness that was astounding. But one felt all the time that she must have been laughing up her sleeve at the absurdity of Lady Carfax and her associates.' So the suppressed instinct percolated through after all!

Arkay also regrets, like his fellow critic on *The Times* that the horsewhippin' Sir Giles does not make any further appearance, remarking: 'So we are only left with these impossibly virtuous, and presumably bad people. The acting did wonders for the play which indeed is of the sorriest stuff . . . The *Knave of Diamonds* belongs to the best beloved of the Kitchen Library, and our own still 'girlish moods'.'

Perhaps the most pleasing description comes from *The Times* which went to town over Violet Vanbrugh's wardrobe, into the design of which much thought and care must have gone, in the hope, perhaps, that when the eye enjoys the mind does not grieve. The descriptions certainly bring the era into focus, and one can visualise Ella in similar finery, but sadly with so small an audience in comparison.

Miss Vanbrugh's Dresses

Miss Violet Vanbrugh's dresses include a beautiful white and gold evening gown worn in the first act, which is draped softly with gold-embossed mousseline-de-soie, the folds being caught at the waist with handsome amber clasps. Over this she wears an evening cloak of pale sunset-blue chiffon velvet held in place with heavy copper and gold tassels, and having an enormous collar of chinchilla and a stole end of the same fur falling over the back. In the same act she dons an embroidered tea-rose pink crêpe-de-chine gown wonderfully embroidered in medallions of gold and royal blue.

This is exchanged, in Act Two, for a dress of mole-coloured crêpe jersey, trimmed with heavy lace in the same colour, the pattern of which suggests carved ivory. For Act Three she has chosen a smart motor frock of lemon coloured cloth, over which she wears a draped cinnamon coloured cloak with a touch of leafgreen galon, the latter colour being repeated in her green leather motoring hat. In Act Four her gown is of soft dove-grey mousseline-de-soie beautifully embroidered.

There is a photograph of Violet in the part, published in *The Tatler* a week later, looking depressed, and far too old for the role of Lady Carfax who was supposed to be twenty-five. Perhaps the strain of so much gentility was grimly ageing. On Thursday, 21st July the play had its 100th performance, and closed shortly afterwards. Ella had been to see a matinee performance, enjoying going backstage afterwards to congratulate Violet on her acting. For Ethel it was enough to listen to Ella's description. She did not admit to worrying about her critics at all; only her public counted, as her readers now numbered millions.

Ethel's next book was taking shape. Working just as hard as usual, she now had a real life model for a hero who had appeared before in *The Obstacle Race*. Charles Rex had intrigued her fans, they wrote and asked her for more about him. Ethel must have thoroughly enjoyed writing about a man after her own heart, however idealised.

That hot summer Peggy and I were given part of the garden fenced off from the rest, where we could be shut in to play safely. It ran beside a field where hay was being cut; some trusses were thrown over, in which we were allowed to scramble and hide. Peggy learnt how to make daisy chains. We crowned each other in white marguerites, or rolled over and over with the white dogs—a hot white summer, we were dressed in white muslin, and white sunbonnets, only our shoes and Peggy's brilliant curls were red.

Down in the fir trees, Ethel paced up and down, hands in pockets, it was cool down there, she did not like either the cries of young children, or the persistent practising of Ella's piano. She was restless and preoccupied.

Ella made me an emerald green elf's outfit, obviously inspired by Cicily M. Barker's book of flower fairies. Cyril Ebsworth came over with Violet, bringing his camera. He took me into the garden and started to take pictures. As it was a very hot day, I struggled out of my costume, and not being discouraged, finally returned to the house holding Cyril's hand, happily in the buff. Nursie was horrified, and Ella highly amused. At three and a half I knew how to feel comfortable— Ella had started directing me onto the path of independent action.

Lady Jane Grey took us all except Ethel to the seaside, where Maurice Bowra joined us, sparing us a precious day or so of his summer vacation from Oxford, to renew his bond with Ella whose advice and council he valued. Her wide reading and catholic tastes never failed to surprise him, she listened so well, paying him the compliment of taking him completely seriously, something she could never do with Ethel, although she worshipped her. While we were away, Ethel, for the first time, took her holiday alone travelling to North Devon. She spent a week tramping the moors, her walking stick her only companion. No one would have recognised the lonely striding figure, hat drawn down over her pale face and anxious eyes, who in a soft husky voice shyly passed the time of day with any locals she met. No photograph of Ethel had ever been published, her identity was still inviolate.

With looks and clothes in mind it might be wondered what occasions Ella found for showing off her spectacular flair for dress. Although she would have dearly loved it, the county did not call, so nothing daunted she set out to meet them on neutral ground, choosing winter sports in Switzerland as her spring board. In the winter of 1921–2, taking Patsy Phillips with her, she stayed at St. Moritz where on Christmas eve, her fabulous mandarin fancy dress won the first prize, a shared excitement as Patsy had been dressed as the mandarin's wife. Her personal originality drew new and interesting friends, mostly women, as men were shy of anyone as independent as Ella. But her pretty young friend came in for much admiration. Both women skiied, but Ella left skating to Patsy, so tall a woman might crash badly, anyway there was no point if she could not excel. Some evenings were taken up with dancing, Ella waltzing Patsy round if she was not already booked with some young man, to the delight of the other guests who apparently accepted Ella as an amusing freak with plenty of money, coupled with a sense of humour. Some evenings were spent wrapped in fur rugs riding in horsedrawn sleighs, which swept along the snowpacked roads, up and up until St. Moritz lay twinkling in the sparkling frost below. At the highest point brandy would be passed round, while the horses steamed and stamped, anxious to descend to their warm stables.

Ethel, left behind at the Greenwood, intended to spend a quiet time on her own. On Christmas Day she went to church at Holy Trinity, Guildford, where she encountered the Savage family in the porch wishing the rector a happy Christmas. They asked her back to Christmas lunch with them, and, to Norah's great satisfaction, she unexpectedly accepted. Ethel had never spent Christmas apart from Ella before, she was sweetly shy, anxious to please, and rather diffident. All Gerald's manly instincts were aroused, he fell headlong into the lovenet which Ethel had so innocently spread. There was no need for Norah to worry any more, what she had hoped for was happening naturally. For Ethel it must have been an enormous relief that the decision was to be taken out of her hands. The hook was truly embedded, she could hold up her head and play it hot or cold at her own discretion, knowing that capitulation was inevitable.

TWELVE

Realities

MERCIFULLY FOR Gerald, Ethel's age did not allow her to protract her dalliance, waiting only until Ella returned from Switzerland to break the news as gently as possible. She sent Lady Jane Grey to Newhaven to retrieve the tourists, with a mysterious letter for Ella, telling her nothing definite, but alerting her to be prepared for a surprise, which of course Ella guessed only too easily.

Ella's immediate reaction was furious jealously of Gerald, whom she did not think worthy of her beloved Nettie. Stalking into the Greenwood, still dressed in a scarlet gabardine skiing habit topped with a black fur hat which she had earlier deliberately donned to amuse Ethel, she confronted her in the hall, a most imposing vision of outraged sisterhood, and according to Nursie the conversation went in the following vein:

'Ethel, where are you?'

'Oh, darling Sissie you're back,' then running downstairs to be checked by the sight of Ella drawn up to her fullest height, holding her letter.

'Gerald, I suppose?' Waggling the letter.

'Oh, yes, yes, it's so wonderful.'

'He's after your money, nothing else.'

'Oh, Sissie, how could you be so cruel?'

'It's kinder to be cruel sooner than later.'

'Gerald loves me.'

'*Pah!*'

Ella stalked off, to change into something more suitable, leaving Ethel running her fingers up and down a blue glass bead necklace, tears in her eyes, a figure of lonely dejection. Nursie came to the rescue; following her into the drawing room, she begged her not to take any notice.

'Miss Ella's very jealous, Miss Ethel, don't you fret, she'll come round.'

I must have watched that scene myself from the landing, Nursie would have had the children ready to welcome Ella home, and it would also account for her presence being unnoticed. Such a private encounter would not knowingly have been enacted in public. Thereafter, Ella dressed in red with a black hat always presaged danger.

In all fairness to Ella, Gerald was by no means a good match for Ethel when considered in the light of his financial standing. He only had his army pay, which was very small when compared to Ethel's affluence. Yet what man could have matched her wealth, running by now at around £30,000 a year? But how many rich men would have wanted a secluded middle-aged virgin with religious ideals, however warmly wrapped in cash? Ethel was a sitting target for any man wanting to enrich his coffers regardless of whether he was suitable or offered any real affection. Gerald could not be condemned on either of these scores, though it took a long time for him to prove this, and in Ella's estimation he never did. Ella wanted too much; equality of income, *and* great love for her sister. Of love she had little experience and of riches only for a very short and recent period in her life. Given her jealous disposition, it was only to be expected that her judgment should be biased. Probably no other man would in the circumstances have been any more acceptable for Ethel than Gerald.

Gerald was thirty eight, only two years younger than Ethel, but this was enough to be an added disadvantage in Ella's eyes. Then what could Gerald know about Ethel? Of how she had to be sheltered from the press, and Ella having organised her life for her, of her total incapacity to run a house? Could she do accounts? Interview servants, and sack employees? Necessary but worldly imperatives, if she was to retain a hold on her independence.

The prospect of Ethel getting married brought with it yet another problem. I could not be divided up, and as Ethel did not care for children, Ella would be obliged to take me on single-handed. There was no adoption law, so Ella arranged for a document to be drawn up which gave her sole right over my future, provided that she herself continued to care for me in a way commensurate to her social standing. As an escape clause, it was stated that if by any chance she should be unable, or unwilling, to continue with the arrangement I could be returned to my mother if she wanted me, or go to a children's home, but with a portion of oil shares for my own untransferable use. My mother saw and signed her copy of this document. Remarkably my mother did not wish for my return, even with oil shares, for which I am eternally grateful, and if she ever reads this, I hope she will be pleased that I realise how unselfish she was to have left me in such an infinitely better situation. How much I would give to meet her, just once, so that she could know I bear her no grudge for anything she might have been forced by her parents to do, all those years ago.

The next consideration was the dogs, those two large white bouncing animals who needed so much attention and exercise. Ethel apparently did not want them, she would have her Gerald, and like any other army wife, should be ready if necessary to move abroad at a short notice. So Una and Henry were taken over by Ella, a welcome outlet for her passion for organising and training; she would lick those spoilt dogs into shape very quickly, and enjoy the doing.

Given the challenge, Ella soon proved that she was well able to readjust her own life, yet at the same time she did not believe that it would ever really be necessary. Ethel did not announce her engagement in the press, preferring privacy for anything so personal, yet it leaked out, to be denied furiously, leading Ella to hope that the situation would eventually resolve itself.

All that winter and early spring, Gerald was a frequent visitor at the Greenwood; he, like Ethel, disliked children, but he also disliked dogs, an aspect of his nature she was to find out later. Norah Savage was very much in evidence, busy making a strong bid for friendship with Ella, getting to know her, and through her all Ethel's little foibles that she could pass on to Gerald to help him in his wooing, a sisterly act which Ella saw through too late, and accused her of false friendship and spying, hurt that Norah's attention had not been entirely for her own beaux yeux. How Ella longed for someone to love her passionately for her own sake, no matter who, she wanted total devotion, unswerving loyalty and admiration. Ella's hope lay with the adoption of myself, but at three and a half I was not much comfort to her at that time, except as a love object with very little emotional response or return for the attention paid me. If the inevitable happened she would have me to herself and this gave her, I hope, a little something to ease the pain of losing Ethel.

For Ethel there was no slacking over her writing. She finished *Charles Rex* ready for spring publication, and dedicated it to Gerald. 'To G.T.S. in remembrance of a winter day.' The book was reviewed by Rebecca West in an article called the Tosh Horse, printed in the *New Statesman* some years later, a very pertinent assessment of the value of writing complete tosh whole-heartedly.

In *Charles Rex*, Ethel makes the mistake, due to ignorance, of letting a supposed cabin 'boy' be both beaten and fondled by Charles Rex. Homosexuality was not a form of love with which she was familiar, apart from the imprisonment of Oscar Wilde, when details were not widely publicised. Ella made the same sort of mistake some years later, befriending a homosexual man and partially supporting him because she sympathised with the difficulties he seemed to have in getting on with people. Once Ella was told the truth she dropped him in horror, and sent him packing. He was never mentioned in the house again. Ethel would have been utterly mystified if her beloved Charles Rex had been accused of interest of an indecent kind in small boys. Yet here in her *New Statesman* article of about 1925 we find Rebecca West referring to *Charles Rex* and saying 'God forbid that any book should be banned, but . . .' and going on to remember that D. H. Lawrence's *The Rainbow*, Lyon O'Neil's *The Cottage Pie*, and *Brute Gods* by Louis Wilkinson did receive this anti-accolade. Miss West also commented that there are those who cannot look at a horse over a hedge, and those who can lead it out through the gate. Ethel led all her horses out through the gate, with only a lump of sugar in her innocent white hand.

Did Ethel know that she was doing this? No, of course not. She was incapable of leading anyone astray, it was entirely a question of innocence lying in the eyes of the beholder. She never imagined that any other motives could be read into her novels than those she meant herself. Was she an ignorant fool?

Ignorant yes, fool no. Foolishness does not embrace enjoyable moral behaviour. Ethel did not shut her eyes to carnal knowledge, but information of that sort did not come her way, and so remained behind a closed door in her mind's experience.

Had Ethel's reader been aware of this, would it have been a let-down? Most of them, and they went into millions, allowed themselves to be led astray by their own knowledge of the world, or equally by their lack of it. Her more imaginative readers put in explanations where she had left them out, and tailored the tales to fit the figures of their own personal experience. Was this why Miss West found herself, to her great surprise, blushing when she read passages from *Charles Rex*, her superior knowledge of human action allowing her to presuppose a situation not intended by the writer?

Leaving the lovers at the bedroom door had been another necessity before marriage, but she continued to do this after the mysteries of lovemaking had been revealed to her, and here one hopes that the reason was taste rather than disillusionment. Every reader has his own personal experience to guide his imagination. Ethel relied implicitly on her public's ability to use this, where she herself could go no further. Lovemaking should be the most private, intimate occupation any of us perform, so why should she later impose her own experience when her previous approach had been so successful?

Even Ella, who adored Ethel, told all her own friends that Ethel's books were 'awful tosh, and not in very good taste', implying that Ella herself had no carnal knowledge, and was a literary snob. True on both counts, although Ella would have been furious to see herself so revealed, and out of her own mouth to wit. . . .

If, as Rebecca West remarks, Ethel had written her novels with good taste as the foremost ingredient, she would never have been so successful as she was—she 'rode the Tosh Horse hell for leather' carrying herself and her readers into runaway flights of fancy. 'No one can write a best seller by taking thought.' There was no room to pander to the Gods of Taste, only sex itself was tastefully evaded, a titillation in itself—why talk about it, what is more distracting than a talkative lover?

No doubt due to her own impending fulfilment, Ethel must have been at her peak period of emotional sentimentality. Ella

could not fail to notice the physical difference in her darling
Nettie. She had put on weight, her cheeks had filled out, and
although her eyes were still ringed in dark shadows, they
looked out with bright anticipation; her mouth smiled more, she
was bright and alert, able to tease Ella with idiotic little practical
jokes, evidently supplied by Gerald. Ethel seemed really happy
for the first time in her life; Ella hoped that it would last if they
married, but the omens did not read well.

Gerald, a lieutenant-colonel in the Royal Army Service Corps,
came from a traditional army family going back several generations, a breed of military engineers, rather than fighters.
Quick to deride anyone she did not like, Ella most unfairly
referred to her future brother-in-law as a Royal Army Scullery-
Maid, a title which Gerald would not have appreciated. Ethel's
own upbringing hardly fitted her for a life devoted to the art of
war. Although several of her imagined heroes had been brave
and glamorous military fighters, the more mundane aspect of
supply, food, arms, transport and equipment had not bothered
her, they were unglamorous functions, they just 'happened'.
Ella must have wondered if Gerald could live up to the glamour
Ethel associated with life in the Army.

Perhaps Gerald's appearance was the draw, after all Ethel had
always been the champion of the unassuming man. With his pale
face, small stature and meagre body, he seemed to be a little
man doing a dull job, but his duty, and doing it well. He had a
disarming grin beneath his ridiculously large moustache,
through which could be seen good white teeth. His taste in
clothes was conservative, but brightened by smart yellow spats,
or sometimes with tartan stockings beneath his baggy plus-
fours. Perhaps Ella's first impression of him, 'Oh Nettie darling,
do be careful, I wouldn't trust a moustache like that', spurred
Ethel to find out if there was any truth in her view, and if
possible to prove her wrong. Whatever the reason, attracted
she was, both protectively and devotedly, and Ella who had
championed her whole life so far, was suddenly left out, and
ignored, a situation she found incomprehensible. No doubt
Chopin's Nocturne No. 5, Op 15, No. 2, had a busy time, a
favourite piece with which Ella frequently consoled herself,
playing with immense feeling, and solemnity.

When it was obvious that the inevitable was going to happen,

Ella pulled herself together, her own favourite expression, both mentally and physically. She would walk tall when she felt it necessary to push her rights, rights which she felt were her due. Where would Ethel be if it had not been for herself? She planned some sort of compensation for being ditched in mid-life.

With great dignity, and helped by the advice of a solicitor, she 'saw' Ethel one morning in the drawing room, pointing out to her that it would be necessary to settle some money on both her siblings before she was finally cast off.

Ethel, of course, had already thought out exactly how much she was going to settle on Reggie and Ella, it all seemed so obvious that it was rather startling to find Ella making the first move, thus pushing her into a defensive attitude rather than the munificent position of enjoying giving away a considerable portion of her accumulated wealth. Ella and Reggie were apportioned £30,000 each. Ella was distinctly chagrined that beloved Nettie should have needed no prompting, and to her amazement was showing better money sense than she had credited to her, a thought which in its turn brought more dark ruminations about any hold she could ever hope to have over Ethel once she was wed and away. That wretched little man was going to be a nuisance, made doubly so by Ella's own firm insistence to Norah Savage that Ethel must be protected from her own too generous inclinations, never suspecting that such a remark could be used to mean from herself, as well as public cadgers.

Nursie knew exactly what was afoot, and had early made up her mind that she would not continue in her position, once Ethel had moved away. Never having liked Ella, the prospect of her unadulterated companionship was not possible to contemplate, quite apart from the different treatment the two children would be accorded once Ethel was not there to see fair play. Nursie began to look around for an alternative occupation which would give her enough money to live an independent life without jeopardising Peggy's future, for which she had high hopes, a beautiful child with brains—which was more than could have been said of myself at that time.

In May 1922, Ethel told her agent, A. P. Watt, what was afoot, and agreed to let it be 'leaked' to the press that she planned to get married on 11th June, and that she would welcome the press that day provided that she was left alone until then. The press left her alone, but for the last time. She did a quite unprecedented thing, possibly the only unkind move in her life, and one which she was to regret at leisure. Ethel persuaded Gerald to obtain a special licence, and early on the morning of 7th June, Ethel drove off with Ella in her Daimler to Holy Trinity Church, Guildford, where she walked down the aisle on the arm of her sister who gave her away at the Altar to be joined in holy matrimony with Gerald, to honour and obey him, in sickness and health. Norah and Gerald's father, a Colonel in the Royal Engineers, sat on his side, and Ella having delivered her lamb to what she was convinced would be slaughter, turned and sat beside Violet Ebsworth, her head held high, lips trembling, and tears pouring down her rose red silk dress. Not even her generously proportioned black hat, trimmed with a trembling rose-coloured ostrich plume, failed to hide her desolation. Nevertheless, she signed the marriage register with a firm hand, she and Gerald's father having been the witnesses.

Lady Jane Grey took the happy pair back to the Greenwood, while in a hired car Norah, her father, Violet Ebsworth, and Ella followed them at a discreet distance. After a quick mid-morning snack, boosted with a bottle of champagne, Ethel and Gerald were away, Ethel had no need to change her clothes, her quietly smart new suit had been carefully chosen to be suitable for her honeymoon exit. Ethel would be forty-one in August; she probably felt that a white wedding might have been absurd— besides what a waste of money, far better to give a donation to the Distressed Gentlefolks association to mark the occasion. By lunch time Ella was alone, if being mistress of such a household could be called that.

Fortunately there was much to arrange. The Greenwood would have to be sold, for she could no longer afford the upkeep of so large a property; besides, it was full of memories. With great courage and initiative she set herself to reorganising her way of living. By the time Ethel and Gerald had consumated their marriage, during a month of total secrecy, telling no one where they were, Ella had found a nice but hardly small country house in the New Forest with some ten acres of land.

When Ethel and Gerald drove over in Lady Jane Grey some six weeks after the wedding they found a small white open car standing outside the Greenwood front door. Gerald saw that it was a Vauxhall 30/98 and whistled through his moustache enviously. Ella had been watching and listening from just inside the porch. Marching down the steps smiling triumphantly, she patted the bonnet, and smiled at Gerald. 'Nice little car isn't she, Gerald, can I take you for a spin?' Ella had taken lessons and was now a competent driver—in her own estimation at least—her new accomplishment giving her more freedom and excitement than anything else that had yet come her way. Ethel was not at all happy, and begged Ella to employ a chauffeur, strongly backed by Gerald who felt he had been upstaged, just as Ella hoped. Ella assured them that a chauffeur was a totally unnecessary expense which she could not afford in any case.

Ethel looked remarkably well, all the better for an enforced holiday, but confided in Ella that her next book was burning to get out, so, as she did not want the bother of running a house, she had persuaded Gerald that for the time being they should live in hotels. Contrary to Ella's hopes he was only too anxious to fall in with his darling Ethel's plans, so for the first two years of marriage they had no home of their own, and were not particularly interested in choosing what they might want from Greenwood, except for the Davenport dessert service which had come down to the sisters from their Granny Parrott. It was a very large service, rather over ornamental in fine bone china, gilded scolloped edges enclosed a wide royal blue border, the centres of each piece painted by a competent hand with different bunches of flowers. Ella wanted to keep it all in one set, but Ethel insisted that Ella should have half. It was meticulously divided up, as were a collection of snuff boxes and vinaigrettes which had belonged to their father.

Ethel's indifference to furniture encouraged Ella to take nearly everything with her to the New Forest, so that most of the good pieces which had come to them through the Parrott connection were kept together. Fortunately Blackmoor, Ella's new house, could amply accommodate them all. Before Ella could move, Reggie's wife gave birth to another son.

Nursie shook her head. She was glad that she was getting out of the family. Ethel was 'sweet magic' but of the other two— 'Now if they had been like Miss Ethel, what a different story.'

THIRTEEN

Looking Back

PERHAPS ETHEL's first tussle with Gerald was over the integrity of her chauffeur who had been with her for ten years. Gerald did not like him, partly, one suspects, because he adored Ethel and would have laid his coat in the mud for her if the opportunity had presented itself, and partly because he knew any servant taken into a new rearranged household resents being given orders by the new 'master'.

Gerald wanted to re-employ his batman from France, Ethel to keep the trusted man she knew so well. One freezing winter's day, with the roads covered in black ice, Gerald gave orders to be taken in Lady Jane Grey to Portsmouth to see Nelson's *Victory*, of which he was making a model. Ethel's driver advised him not to go, it was dangerous. Gerald told him he must be a rotten driver if he could not cope with a little ice, and insisted on his taking the car out. Ethel heard the argument and immediately put on her coat, telling them that she would go as well, hoping thus to put a stop to the trip. But this was just what Gerald wanted, he called her bluff, and off they went. The chauffeur, thoroughly unnerved by Gerald's bullying, drove slowly and nervously, took a downhill corner with his brakes locked, skidded into a tree, and turned the car over. Ethel was thrown against a window pillar, and her face very badly cut. Gerald, nearly out of his mind with anger and distress, sacked the wretched man on the spot.

Ethel bore the scar for the rest of her life, a deep gash across her right cheek, which embarrassed her, emphasising her natural shyness. What Gerald never knew was that Ethel gave her ex-chauffeur a pension for life, and an excellent recommendation; she was well aware of the cause of the accident.

Apart from his chagrin over Ethel, Gerald was delighted to have the field clear so that Tom Blomfield, his ex-batman, could take over. While Ethel was recovering from the accident, and by the time she was ready to go out for a drive again, Tom had mastered Lady Jane Grey who had suffered very little damage. Tom was a very competent driver and mechanic, with a pleasant manner, which never overstepped into familiarity; he was rank and file, Gerald was an Officer, never to be forgotten for an instant. Ethel liked him at once, later relying on him to take care of her when the press were tiresome. Tom would press a button on the dashboard which would automatically let down blinds in the passenger's compartment if ever he saw reporters on the prowl. Cars in those days were driven with the chauffeur sitting outside in the cold, able to communicate with the passenger only by speaking tube. On picnics he would stand guard, out of earshot but near enough to warn them of intruders.

Ethel's first year of marriage produced *Tetherstones* and a now very rare little book of verse, both published by Hutchinson. Ethel was no poet, she has never been included in any anthology, but it must be admitted there was a feeling and talent, especially in 'Stones' which was included both in the book of verse and on the first page of *Tetherstones*, a book which she dedicated to Violet Ebsworth, 'The dear friend who always stands by, as a token of my ever loving gratitude for all she has done for me'. *Tetherstones* seems to be written as a memorial to the days at Greenwood, a tale to reveal the kind of life from which she had moved away, and the existence she was now embarking upon. It is a book of Hail and Farewell. The only person to cross the stream with her and receive welcome unbounded, was Violet Ebsworth, her loved friend, counsellor and comforter in times of need. She was indeed the most deserving choice for its dedication.

Tetherstones was written entirely in hotel bedrooms, or bathrooms. Wherever they stayed, a private suite was engaged, giving Ethel the necessary privacy; if a maid came in to do the room, she moved into the bathroom, and back again as necessary. All meals were served in the room, she did not go into public rooms at all, so it is doubtful if the other residents knew of her existence other than as Major Savage's retiring wife. Divorced from the overpowering atmosphere which Ella created around herself, Ethel was able to take off into the realms of fiction far more easily; she could think about her past life with detachment, no longer having to fight to be herself, or to be Ella's younger sister escaping in order to be alone. Ethel's situation was of her own pleasurable choosing, her solitude ceased to bear the overtones of guilty escapism and she could enjoy it with a clear conscience.

As a celebration of Ethel's release from her previous life, *Tetherstones* deserves careful study, particularly since all the characters have their counterpart in real life. The book has an excellent skeletal structure covered in the muscles and tissues of reality, spoilt only by Ethel's usual exaggerations, and over-drawn characters. She was still so unsure of herself and her potential that she felt impelled to over-emphasise, not realising that the reader could fill in and use his own imagination. Ethel had to spell it all out, panting the while.

Frances, the downtrodden middle-aged secretary in poor health, but blessed with artistic leanings and a noble pure courageous spirit, must be Ethel herself, or perhaps how she visualised what her own reactions would have been given the circumstances of the story.

The Bishop of Burminster one is tempted to transpose into Ella, pushing, relentless of detail, trampling on human frailty, and very self-centred in the name of God (which in Ella's case would have been class-consciousness). Taking only Ella's worst aspects can be forgiven, when it is remembered that Ethel had only just escaped her clutches, and was probably still smarting from the lashings of her tongue towards her marriage. Should anyone who knew Ella detect the similarity, the imagery had served its purpose. Ethel was too gentle a person to be vindictive, but her strong sense of right behaviour had been bruised by Ella's apparent indifference to her future once she had left home.

Montague, the Bishop's nephew, must have been her brother Reggie, a weak, selfish charmer, who found it easy to take all and give very little back, yet he too has a better side to his character which is discovered by Frances. Even this, however, does not attract her enough nor does she find it sufficiently spiritual to ensnare her heart.

Ruth, the angelic baby girl, blind and in touch with God, is a physical mixture of Peggy and myself—Peggy with her marvellous flaming curls, elegant and beautifully formed body, myself very plain, short-sighted and unable to look up at light so that most photographs of me as a small child make me look blind. The Godly part was entirely imagination, Ella never having approved of religious teaching, except for an apology for a prayer at night time *in* bed. The other parts of the character were taken from real life; I was woefully independent, pressing my love on all comers, a dreamer of visions, a wanderer, yet anything but an angel. I remember getting into bed with any grown-up who would have me, particularly with Ethel, who was not so demanding as Ella, and listened patiently to my non-senses. Nursie had been very disapproving, another reason for her wishing to move on; she would never have allowed Peggy to wander about the house unchecked. Clearly, I was going to be a bad influence very soon.

Arthur is Gerald, Ethel's treatment of the good man under pressure from his family, yet even Arthur's tendency to cruelty is so tenderly handled that Frances' great love for this awkward, endearing man shines through even the most unpleasant scenes. Frances chose him as her great love, just as Ethel did Gerald in real life.

In Arthur's six sisters, some of the Greenwood women have been immortalised. From them Ethel is taking her farewell in the only way she knew how, by letting them re-live some of the incidents that brought them most to her mind. Slight portraits, but true.

Maggie—'Rosy, rough haired, good with cows', is Vivian Philips, who when at home almost lived for her goats. She had a tanned skin which blushed easily, and her hair was wild and dark.

Dolly—'A girl of considerable character, and decision, with an aptitude for nursing' was Evelyn Vidler, the daughter of their Ashford doctor, who had helped nurse both their father and mother when they were dying.

Nell—'Twenty, always had hay seed sown in her chestnut hair, full of ideas, an original, delightfully and naively human', could only have been Patsy Philips.

Lucy—'easily frightened, with a shy and gentle way with her', Edith de Wolf, old school friend, ugly, kind and diffident, tied to her old mother.

Milly—'sensitive, anxious to please, not very strong or

capable, but always full of sympathy and never failing attention', Mary Bastard, another old school friend and a wasted beauty, also tied to an antique mother.

Elsie—'of the boisterous open air type, capable of doing a man's labour on the farm, "I'm used to broken nights, Maggie, and I come in for them in lambing time".' This is, I think, Madge Phillips before her marriage, and is the only character of whose identity I am not sure.

Arthur's mother was a composite person, Mrs. Coombs, the sad little cook, and also an evocation of Ethel's own mother, with her white banded hair and her sighs.

Oliver is a genuinely fictitious character, possibly inspired by an under-gardener who had a soft spot for one of the Greenwood maids.

What follows is a summary which may not perhaps do justice to a singularly complicated story, running in the original to 95,000 words.

The heroine of *Tetherstones* is Frances, a sad-eyed, middle-aged delicate spinster, who is the overworked secretary of the Bishop of Burminster. When Frances meets his nephew, Montague, he unexpectedly falls for her; the Bishop discovers them in his garden at night and indignantly expels them both, God throwing out Adam and Eve with a warning. Frances goes for a holiday; Montague finds her, and first she allows much kissing, then repents and goes off for a walk. She loses her way, only to be led still further astray by Montague, with whom she finds herself marooned at night in a cattle-shed. Montague is about to take advantage of the situation, when the blind child, Ruth (Angel of God?), appears and conducts her back to safety. She develops fever from her soaking on the moors, is nursed back to health in the home which Arthur, a farmer, shares with his six sisters. As Frances slowly recovers she realises that she loves Arthur protectively, but he is a violent man, and senses her past with Montague who is still trying to see her. Going out into the night in a rage, Arthur is involved in a shooting fracas with Montague, who persuades Frances to accompany him to London. There Frances hopes to sell her sketches, while Montague, who has been wounded, needs her attention. Frances now has time to think about Arthur; his directness shocks her, but his love moves her to the depths.

But yet she knows—as we all know—that it is not by time or any other circumstance that Love the Immeasurable can be measured, and that no power on earth can ever obliterate the memory of love.

Arthur alone had entered the shrine of her heart. She could not cast him aside however hard she tried.

After a night with Montague, binding his wound and sleeping in separate rooms, she waits, weeping, for her fate. Deliverance however is nigh. News arrives that the Angel child Ruth is dangerously ill and calling for her. Frances prays for help, not really wanting to return to the farm and its turbulent owner, but since her heart is true and sound, she decides to return, saying to herself that she is just 'driftwood—driftwood'. Oliver, the farm hand, tells her that Arthur is extremely upset about the child but would rather die than show it. Frances' heart goes out to him. The description of the Devonshire moors is, incidentally, excellent and must have been noted when Ethel had her holiday there the year before.

Frances finds Ruth dying with her eyes 'open'; she had fallen at the Tetherstones on the moor, that fateful place so full of mystery where she herself had so nearly come to 'grief' with Montague. Frances realises that Ruth is still acting as God's messenger, the burning sightless eyes remind her of those of the Bishop of Burminster when he cast Montague and herself out of his garden. Ruth says she has a message, yet everyone waits for the Angel of Death. While waiting, Frances goes down and has tea with Arthur's old father, a scholarly recluse who is bullied by his son. He is writing a book on the history of Tetherstones, but Arthur's mother comes in, and Frances escapes to the kitchen where she finds Arthur in lonely despair and, not frightened of him any more, comforts him. (A very good moving scene, but rather spoilt by drinking tea and eating toast—possibly intended to symbolise Bread and Wine.) Frances ruminates:

> In that hour she knew that she was chained indeed, beyond all hope of escape. Brute beast as he described himself—murderer at soul as she believed him to be—yet he had implanted that within her soul which she could never cast out. Whatever he was, whatever he did, could make no difference now. She loved him.

Arthur's father has heart trouble which affects his brain (like Ethel's own father), while Arthur (like Ella) resents his father. Arthur says,

'I have wished him dead for years—why should I be sorry—he who all my life has stood in the way of my gaining anything I hold worth having—my chances are gone.'

This makes Frances (for reasons I cannot fathom) feel that the Stones are turning to bread. . . .

Arthur's father, his mind wandering, mistakes Frances for a long dead daughter (Ruth's mother), then comes back to reality again, a scene which is very well handled. So is the episode where Arthur's sister Maggie returns from market married to Oliver, the farmhand, without having asked Arthur's permission. Arthur orders them out of the house. When Oliver says 'No one will ever love you, Arthur,' Frances to her own amazement, stands up and says 'Oh yes, I will'. Ethel unfortunately spoils this simple effect by making Frances 'turn to him quivering with all the greatness of the occasion to find his eyes upon her with that in them that thrilled her to the soul'. Later 'her pride comes back to her, and she lifted it grandly like a banner'.

Splendid stuff but it has a cooling effect on Arthur as they pace the dark garden together. Frances declaiming:

'When I say love I don't mean the mere physical attraction which so many mistake for love, I mean the holy thing, the love of the spirit which nothing can ever change or take away. That is too sacred to be tampered with, and no third person should ever presume to touch it. It comes from God and should command our utmost reverence—even homage.'

Arthur being a little tongue-tied after this announcement, manages to pour out the love of his whole soul—'the perfect gift'—in one word: 'Frances'.

In spite of this astonishing gift, Frances goes off to London. On arrival there, she is unexpectedly met by Montague, he takes her to dinner, to a theatre and thence to his flat. Frances realises her whereabouts only when he locks the door. She turns on him with the words, 'You hound'. He does not argue the point, and asserts that now he's got her he will conquer her. Frances faints, a serviceable habit which she used before to

avoid facing tiresome situations. When she recovers she tells
him that if he 'takes her, she will never see him again as she will
be dead'. Montague agrees to let her go. At that moment the
door bell rings and she is pushed unwillingly into his bedroom to
hide.

Arthur rampages in, fights Montague, and Frances rather unexpectedly tells him that Montague's behaviour has been
'honourable', because she has promised to marry him in the
future. Arthur departs in fury while she repeats to herself 'It's
dead, it's dead', presumably meaning Arthur's love for her.
Montague, never one to miss an opportunity, makes another bid
for Frances, but humbly this time. She pities him and says, 'The
fault was mine. I always knew in my heart—that you were—
that sort of man.' 'My god,' said Montague, 'You've haven't
much mercy.' To which Ethel adds the rider, 'Not by strength,
and not by strategy, but purity of heart did she conquer the devil
in his soul'.

A vision of Ruth, the blind child, leads Frances back to her
hotel where a telegram from the Bishop summons her back to
work. Without hesitation she obeys. Back in the Bishop's
garden, she finds Montague, who has challenged Arthur to a
duel.

Frances goes to the Tetherstones, where the duel is to be
fought. Arthur's old father in his madness thinks Frances and
Arthur are Ruth's mother and her lover, so he blows up the
Rocking stone in an effort to kill them. Instead he kills himself.
Frances fearing the victim must be Arthur, prays to his spirit,
but the real Arthur materialises, and all is well for ever and ever.

Tetherstones was mostly written in Hertford, where Gerald
was stationed. Undoubtedly she was happy there, or else she
would not, sixteen years later and already a sick woman, have
left her home and returned to Hertford to keep Gerald company.
Clearly, she wished to remember those first two years of
marriage.

The momentous question—was her marriage happy once her
imagined lovemaking became a reality?—can be answered
without hesitation: yes, extremely. Perhaps not ecstatically,

since she was neither excitable nor demonstrative, nor was she given to admitting or showing her passion in public. How, then, could she have written such purple passages? Ethel needed a medium and a catalyst, to demonstrate her understanding of emotions. She had had plenty of experience of scenes with both Ella and her father. Most strongly felt emotions can be channelled into reverse, from hate to love, from fear to trust, from jealousy to generosity if the manipulative power is available, and Ethel had this power. She could imagine man in fury, his outward uncontrolled demonstration very like that of a man frustrated in love. She knew, too, how to control a woman's fear of that man, the knocking of the knees which can be cured by simply 'standing tall', and pretending to trust in his 'better self', thus turning the tables and the tide, putting the onus onto the wrongdoer. This seemed Ethel's answer to any situation that threatened to be getting out of control.

Ethel loved Gerald very much. She had draped him around her little finger much as Frances had Arthur sewn up and tamed, yet not so crudely that he was aware of it. Ethel enjoyed playing the part that she had so often written about; she put her theories into practice and they worked well.

Could Ethel herself let go and enjoy lovemaking? I am sure she could, provided that it happened safely under the wings of the Church and the law of the land, the former more important to her than anything else. Not that she was a moraliser, she had far too light a touch to risk boring people with righteousness, and could laugh at herself with no illusions about how she herself appeared to the world. To her dying day, she looked like a spinster; her sense of humour and the distinct twinkle in those dark blue eyes betrayed a hidden Ethel whom Gerald alone knew, and that, as she would have said, was as it should be.

Why should she bother to glamorise herself physically when she had all that she wanted in a devoted and adoring husband, let alone the great worldy success which rather embarrassed her?

Had she thought that her books were being read and *misunderstood*, she would certainly have stopped writing. Like a missionary, she preached the ideal existence and peopled her stories with both good and bad, the former always winning through in the end against immense odds.

Nowadays we are all so sophisticated and knowing, that much

of her innocent writing is rather embarrassing. To Ethel sex was totally pure (provided that you had the right to enjoy it) and to this degree she was ahead of her time. Her own up-bringing was hardly a garden of pleasure, so one is left with the conclusion that Ethel must have been a passionate saint, taking passionate in its physical meaning. She had apparently no difficulty in reconciling the one characteristic with the other.

FOURTEEN

Two Houses

GERALD WAS the fourth son in a family whose military inheritance had been passed down from father to son in an unbroken line for one hundred years. He followed suit as expected, and although his career in the R.A.S.C. was not so glamorous as those of his father and elder brother, who were in the sappers, he had acquitted himself bravely and honourably during the Great War. When he was in charge of a huge Army repair depot at Rouen, his father, visiting him from the front, remarked that Rouen, with its continual raids, was almost more unpleasant than the skirmishes he himself had been experiencing on the battle line. Organising the rescue of his men from a burning oil store at great personal risk and courage helped Gerald to earn his D.S.O. Always a cheerful wag, his jokes were sometimes not very good, but it took courage to josh at all under continual air-raids and bombardment. None of the Savage men were ambitious, they were first class soldiers, paying attention to duty and leadership, but the first love of all the others was music, which meant more to them than the sound of gunfire. Wherever they went, their cellos or violas went too. The exception was Gerald, who was not musical at all. He was to be an exception in another way, too. When he had been at Hertford for about eighteen months he was commissioned to go to India. His astonishment and possibly relief can be imagined when Ethel put her long elegant hand down firmly on the table and said NO. None of the Savages liked going abroad, and in this respect Gerald was like the rest of them. To refuse a commission meant giving up his career, and for Gerald, a military man who had reached the rank of lieutenant colonel, it was an irrevocable step. But Ethel had her way and Gerald left the Army, remaining only on the reserve of officers.

One might have expected her, of all people, to have welcomed a personal look at the settings of so many of her novels. Yet she could not bring herself to face the difference between what she had imagined and the truth. The chance of disparity between her own descriptions and the facts was too great a risk to run, so Ethel kept her own India inviolate.

Gerald resigned his commission, and devoted the rest of his days to doing nothing in particular, except to make and play with model boats and steam engines. A member of the Savage family says that there is a streak of laziness in their make-up; Gerald evidently had a liberal dose. Except for some useful voluntary organising for the Winchester hospitals some years later, he never did another stroke of work.

It must have been demoralising for him to find that there was no need to make money. To be able to rely on your wife to keep you must undermine your self-esteem. Gerald's complacent acceptance of the situation evidently irritated his family. Never great at getting together, they tended to drop him; all but one, his sister Norah, who adored him. She was his guide and confidante for as long as she lived, pursuing a dangerous and rocky path between Ethel and Gerald, yet loving and being a friend to both without interfering. A considerable achievement. For Ethel, Norah's friendship with her presaged danger from Ella's jealousy, but she could risk it safely at that distance. The two sisters fundamentally adored each other, so Ella's real dislike of Norah hurt and distressed Ethel. Her enjoyment of Norah was always tinged with a feeling of disloyalty towards Ella.

During 1924, Gerald and Ethel found exactly the house for which they had been so unhurriedly looking. Little Woolpit, Pitch Hill, Ewhurst, and here they settled for several years, making a few friends who lasted them for life. Here Gerald, who was clever with his hands, built his first miniature scale model railway. It chuffed round the garden, Tom Blomfield shovelling coal like mad, with Gerald sitting crouched and uncomfortable, but ecstatically happy, at the controls; one hand was always free to wave at anyone who cared to watch the fun.

There is no doubt that they were very happy. If Gerald felt lonely, he took Tom with him on a trip. They shared the excitement of trying out the various model ships, motor boats, and experimental mechanical refinements for which Gerald had such a flair; it was said that Ethel was occasionally persuaded into sitting on the railway truck, just for one trip, but this could only have been to humour Gerald, it was not her scene at all. Their happiness was not in doing things together; that would have been too competitive. Simply knowing that they were near each other was sufficient, even if their actual occupations were poles apart.

Even in her happiness Ethel did not feel inspired to unfetter her imagination on fashionable clothes. She dressed as always in sombre colours, with skirts a little too long for fashion, plain silk blouses, and desperately sensible shoes.

A young woman artist, a friend of one of Ethel's local Ewhurst acquaintances, was allowed to sketch in the courtyard where Ethel and her hostess were sitting talking and knitting; she had begged for at least a glimpse of the distinguished guest. The shock of seeing the writer of such thrilling novels as *The Way of an Eagle* and *The Bars of Iron*, dressed so drably and *knitting* was intense, and a sad disillusionment. Ethel seemed plain too, with big feet, and had never even been to India. This may well have been why Ethel avoided the Press, realising what a disappointment she would be to her fans.

That she never bored her readers must have been due in part to her sincerity. She firmly believed in her heroes, her heroines and in every word she wrote. How else could she have been swallowed whole by so large a part of the English public? Ethel did, as Rebecca West described it at the time, ride her Tosh Horse with a good firm seat, enjoying every minute of it, especially when she could whip up the speed into a hell-for-leather gallop.

Quiet, gentle, sweet-tempered Ethel, what furies you kept at bay in your spinsterish breast, furies that included delight in chastisement, be it self-inflicted or masochistic scenes of beatings, whippings, and flailings. The enthusiasm with which she described such events (and all of them her own creation) makes it a wonder that she is never known to have slapped a child, raised a hand in wrath, or shouted. Did she know that her favourite food, steamed eels, had to be battered to death down at the fishmongers in Winchester? Were her wicked and delicious enjoyments taken in this way, or did she long for Gerald to beat her? Gerald could swear imaginatively, but if Ethel ever heard him do so she would leave the room, or close a window to shut out such an offensive sound.

Over at Blackmoor, Burley, in the New Forest, Ella was busy entertaining and learning to ride. Patsy Phillips had become part of the household, and was given the task of setting up a small stud stables for hunters. Her responsibilities extended to teaching both Ella and me to ride. When it became known that Ella liked chestnut mares, every gipsy in the New Forest who could lay hands on an orange coloured horse brought him up the drive to show off, and hopefully sell. All manner of broken-down animals arrived, and Patsy was kept busy inspecting their teeth, legs and gait. Eventually a big hunter was brought in, which was in good condition, and said to be mild as milk. Patsy rode her round, thought she might be suitable for Ella, and after much haggling, bought her for £80, a large sum in those days.

Ella refused to ride sidesaddle, considering it too elegant and feminine; she thought that a large-boned woman would look better astride, so a special saddle was made for her in Ringwood. A tailor cut her a masterly riding coat, dividing elegantly at the back to hang down over her thighs which were not Ella's pride. But what Patsy had not realised was Ella's fear of horses, a fear that any sensitive horse will pick up immediately, and very often play up to.

Ella's desire to ride stemmed from my own great enthusiasm, I had been given a shetland pony as soon as I could balance on a donkey's back, and in 1924 was already on to my first small hunter, riding to hounds with Patsy who was a martinet as a teacher. Ella would dearly have loved to go out riding with me, but her nervous tension communicated itself to every horse she tried; she was thrown twice, and run away with once, and then decided that it was better to stay on the ground, excel with her piano and singing, cultivate her beautiful garden, and drive fast cars. Ella and horses did not go together.

Ethel came to stay for a whole week one summer—perhaps Gerald was away in camp—and I remember her visit very clearly. She was smothered by the dogs, Una and Henry, who had not seen her for several years. They leapt all over her, licking her face, whining with pleasure, and making wild dashes round the garden and back, to start the display all over again. Ethel's love of dogs must have been one of the few aspects of his wife that Gerald really disliked; she never owned a dog after marriage, yet her ability to gain their confidence and affection was remarkable. In the short time she was with us, she had persuaded Patsy's cocker spaniel bitch Pipperty, a nervous and elderly mother of many litters, that it would be fun to sit on the saddle of my shetland pony and be trotted around the garden. Good as she herself was with animals, Patsy could hardly believe her eyes.

Ella made the most of having Ethel to herself. They spent long hours walking round the garden, Ella showing off her treasures and new acquisitions. The formal garden ran down to the main paddock where several ponies would be shirking about hoping for a lump of sugar. The large kitchen garden backed onto the stables and garage where a large arbutus shrub dropped ripe strawberry-like fruits onto the ground; it was fun to squash them underfoot, making a delicious looking creamy-pink paste round the soles of my shoes. Ella scolded me, but Ethel agreed that it was rather fun. The apiary was a forbidden area. Thatcher, the head gardener, alone ruled supreme here, though he allowed Ethel to go very close and watch the bees coming and going. 'They won't hurt *you*, Mum' he said, which annoyed Ella, who always had to be kept at a safe distance.

Then there were the madonna lilies, massed in front of a tall dark yew hedge. A stiff awe-inspiring sight, their white trumpets breathed out a sickly scent and yellow tongues dropped a sticky sulphurous dust on my head if I tried to reach up to touch the white fleshy petals. Ethel repeatedly stood and looked at them, as if she wanted to take an impression of their stately beauty away with her.

Ethel's public were reading at this time *The Unknown Quantity* written during the second year of her marriage. Both dialogue and characterisation show a more mature hand and there are some delightful cockney passages without the faintest hint of snobbery which are of almost Dickensian quality. A dominant, brazen, bossy society woman with an interfering nature and a heart of gold could well be a mixture of Ella and Norah.

Somehow her heroine quite credibly collects seven proposals in four days and Ethel even invents a two page sermon without moralising. Riding her Tosh Horse, yes, but with much greater confidence—there are no runaway gallops and beatings are down to threatened smacks. There is unusual imagery too: of church bells, 'a door swinging to and fro between them and the world', and an acoustic observation, 'it does me good to hear you smile.'

There is an excellent description of backstage, early in the morning at a London theatre, draughty, with cleaners, carpenters, and a safety curtain that has stuck. This must have been first-hand experience, gleaned from the stage production of her book *The Way of an Eagle* which had opened in June 1922 while she was on her honeymoon.

Perhaps once she was engaged to be married she felt freer to go to London and see what was being done to her famous first book. That *The Way* had gone through forty five editions before it was turned into a play did not help the production, which although it ran at the Adelphi for longer than her previous play *The Knave of Diamonds*, and had Godfrey Tearle as its star, received for the most part disparaging press notices such as 'The scene is supposed to be laid in India, a land which demands a somewhat special knowledge' (*The Times*). Since the book had been written ten years before, and a bloody war had intervened, the Edwardian language and the Indian inaccuracies were all the more readily jumped upon.

The Times also remarked 'It gets itself along by the methods of a novel rather than of the stage, with an excess of (rather flat) talk, and a defect of dramatic concentration. But there is plenty of (rather crude) melodrama for those who like it, which the 'Adelphi' public may be trusted to do, and certainly, from the cheers, did last night.' Another intellectual washing of the hands, this time perhaps flavoured with a little envy.

Sir John Gielgud when asked about her plays, wrote to me saying: 'I well remember the Ethel M. Dell craze, of course, and a dramatisation of the *Way of an Eagle* at the old Adelphi.' Ethel was indeed a craze, and Ella, walking her quietly around the garden, may have felt an angry awe of this unusual sister of hers. Never much at ease with her after her marriage, Ella began to feel excluded from all the public glamour and increasingly jealous of Gerald. Ella was never again to have her sister to herself for a whole week, and perhaps anticipating this she invited the Vanbrugh sisters over for part of the time.

Violet Ebsworth and her brother came too; it was a gathering of old friends, and after dinner Ella's voice rang out over the empty terraced garden, a deep resonantly rich sound. Upstairs in my night nursery I woke up and listened.

Ethel was writing at this time *A Man Under Authority* which she dedicated to 'My dear friend Violet Vanbrugh, in loving remembrance of 1921'. With this novel Ethel begins with a Jane Austen flavour of gossip and carping, introducing a heroic unmarried vicar, who is inclined to have an arch sense of humour, but is especially nice to elderly spinsters. This story must surely have been written with a particularly devoted section of Ethel's readership in mind, as quite half of her fan mail consisted of effusive appreciations from that downtrodden part of the post-war public, the 'lady companions', whose nearest approach to romanticism was via the written word.

The flowering of the Greenwood aloe takes an important role. She bestows on it magic and an ability to bring good luck. That it flowered during the year she met Gerald may have given the phenomenon special significance. There is no doubt that Ethel must have stood quietly in the moonlight and studied the aloe, but can one detect an element of fear? 'Its spearlike leaves flung strange fantastic shadows before him, and he halted with the whimsical thought that some spell might fall upon him if he trod where they lay.' That she could let a vicar, a man of God, think such a thing would excuse such a fantasy which could hardly be called Christian, any more than the descriptive effects of meeting a beautiful woman close by this magical aloe. 'There was a fragrance other than mere English flowers in the air— a maddening elusive essence to which his whole being pulsed in fiery uncontrolled response.' A modern interpretation of this passage would be of suggestive vulgarity. Ethel was married when she wrote it, but even if the idea was carnal, it sprang from her soul not her body. Ethel and her heroines did not have carnal bodies, it was their beautiful souls which caused all the romantic damage.

Are vicars more romantic than most men, does their calling and pure daily life leave them more vulnerable when confronted with a seductive beauty? According to the books of Ethel, yes. '"Circe!" he whispered. "Circe!" and he knelt scarcely knowing what he did, and kissed the wet sweet earth on which her feet had been resting.' Oh angelic Tosh Horse, moonlight gallops evidently fertilise fantastic phenomena! Ethel encapsulated reality in a cocoon of conceit in much the same way that she ate dreary, stewed rhubarb, but enthusiastically topping it over with meringue, and since the eels she so much enjoyed had been dealt with by the fishmonger, she could enjoy their flagellated carcases without a thought. Ethel armed herself with a sword of honour, which she kept well sharpened, yet never drew; there was no need—the scabbard was constructed of transparent crystal. Ethel invites one to trip upon her carefully laid garden path in any way open to the imagination and herein perhaps lies her appeal, the onus of the interpretation being left squarely with the reader.

Perhaps the nearest arrival at contemporary comment 'one of your smart dressed up women of fashion, that spend their lives powdering their noses and polishing their fingernails' can be traced not to Ethel but to Ella; as I read the passage I felt I could hear her voice. Of the future, 'they will be going barefooted and polishing their toenails next' is perfectly accurate, as is a comment about long-haired girlish men and bob-haired boyish girls. Ethel was perspicacious too: 'Personally she did not like him much, but she considered him to be aristocratic and tolerated him in consequence.' This again could have been Ella's feeling about some of her county neighbours.

Ethel's realisation that she herself was a romantic par excellence is confirmed where she remarks of one of her less enchanting characters, 'and if romance were lacking she had not the imagination to miss it greatly'. She was clearly aware that much of what she wrote was made of the stuff of dreams. One wonders how much Ethel herself missed romance in her own life. If she gave Gerald a rose, did he eagerly press it in his pocket book? One hopes for her sake that he did, but with his military background and stern upbringing, one fears that his word for such an act would have been 'soppy'.

About that time, my own forays into the world of green-coated huntsmen in the New Forest were abruptly brought to a halt by Ella, to whom Patsy had vividly described the cornering and death of a stag. This shocked and disgusted her and she had no intention of allowing me to be exposed to such deliberate cruelty.

This scene finds its way into *A Man Under Authority* in a rather naïve form. The heroine, exposed as a suspected murderess, assumes the shocked and terrified look of a cornered doe. Had Ethel written 'doe' it would have been more suitable, but she forgot to change the sex and the beautiful heroine becomes a stag.

Where action slackens off Ethel displays a new-found ability to pad, filling the page with gratuitous and non-pertinent information which was pleasant enough to read, but did nothing to forward the story. Harder to accept was her insistence on the power of confession and absolution as practised by the Church of England. She makes her hero cast out devils with the greatest of ease, yet her public were not deliberately being given passion wrapped in leaves from the Gospels to make it acceptable. Ethel's own belief in God was so strong that all her tales seem designed to leave the reader with a mental exclamation mark, not of doubt or scepticism, but of pleasant surprise that it all had been possible. There is no attempt to be clever at the expense of faith, which shines through all her work; most irritatingly at times, like the parson who said 'There is no chance of making a mistake when we know that He will be our Guide, even unto death'. Ethel does not leave much room for argument. Faith has no concrete reason, and cannot be explained; nor does Ethel try to do so. After certain passages the reader may feel—well there may be something in it after all. May this not be her message, a message of hope to all those whom she considered lost in the dark, without love or comfort?

Ethel obviously enjoyed writing *A Man Under Authority* and revels in the lyrical love affair of the heroic parson with a lady of doubtful virtue, and in proving her innocence and purity of heart, never forgetting of course the beauty of her soul. Not a book for all-comers, as her previous novels had been. There is a time when every author reveals the driving reason why he writes, and this must be the book which Ethel wrote as much for herself as for her 'lady companion' fans.

FIFTEEN

High Output

THE GREATEST struggle that Ethel fought with both her public and her publishers was for personal privacy. Married life made her more vulnerable, she could not use 'the Cassan' as her stand-in, and when it was necessary to stay at hotels, she posed as Gerald's sister, and they took single rooms. It is probable that they sought a house in the country for this reason. Ethel's sojourn in the hotel at Hertford was long enough to have aroused suspicion.

How hard it must have been for Gerald to forgo telling his brother officers who his wife was, but forgo it he did as may be gathered from the short story *The Passer-by* which was published in 1925, in time for the May clutch of new books.

Credit that Ethel remained anonymous must go to her agent, A. P. Watt, who jealously guarded her secret, knowing how much privacy meant to her. The reasons for this are so well expressed in the story, that we can hear Ethel herself explain, as she does in the heroine's words. While it was being written $50,000 was being offered by American publishers for her portrait, and no doubt Gerald knew this, even before they were married. It was said that he himself was frequently offered great sums of money for a snapshot, or even a hint as to where a photographer might lie in wait for her. His reaction to this type of approach can be imagined from a description by one of their maids of what would happen: 'He used to swear at them like a trooper, tell them to get off the property, and then shout after them, "Don't fall over the step and break your leg".'

Their servants were constantly plagued, and there were frequent attempts at bribery. But not one person who knew her ever gave her away. They all fell under her spell, and were truly loyal, behaving like Dell heroes; bravely protective yet unassuming, they denied themselves great riches, donned angel's armour, and fought off the evil spirits with swords of honour.

Ethel's own view is spoken by an imaginary artist in the same predicament as herself. Calling herself her own aunt, she says,

'My aunt is a plain woman, and she feels as I do, that to be made a show of would be—quite intolerable. She considers all self-advertisement is vulgar, and she—she would never stoop to it.'

'It's rather selfish of her,' said Guy.

This was a view held by most of Ethel's public, who passionately wanted to meet their heroine, convinced as they were that she must always be writing about herself. This aspect comes into the story. Guy challenges the artist and she denies it, saying that the portrait is not of herself. 'Oh, but it was never meant, never intended, that picture was just a fancy, nothing else. It is not in the least like me, B . . . is fair, and I am dark.' Then there is a rather charming admission on Ethel's part, as she allows the artist to enquire, 'Do you like it?' and when Guy says that he does, she laughs and says,

'I am glad of that. But you are not one of the great public who hunt the lions? I mean you would never care who painted it? You are not the kind.'

There was a hint of anxiety in her look.

'I care much more for the picture than the artist,' said Guy bluntly.

Her face cleared. 'I knew you would. Now let us talk of something else.'

So from subterfuge to subterfuge, from niece alias aunt to sister alias sister-in-law. Ella, living in Burley, was frequently mistaken for Ethel; her initials were only one letter wrong, and being more outgoing and glamorous, she attracted a fair amount of attention, frequently being pointed out as 'There goes Ethel M. Dell'. Even as a small girl of six I had my share of being pestered for my Aunty's picture, but having been forewarned I was either rude or pretended not to understand. I was told that Auntie Ethel wrote silly books that were not worth reading, so I never did until I started to write this biography. Ella kept a few of them in her spare room, all sentimentally inscribed in Ethel's own hands on the fly-leaf. *The Passer-by* has 'For my own darling Elizabeth, with very best love as always from her

Nettie'. Although Ethel had used one of Ella's true names, she always called her 'Sissie darling' to her face, and occasionally in her dedications as well.

Ethel created her stories out of the world of make-believe, marrying them to fact which she had experienced only through reading of them in the press. Personal experience played little part in the process until well after she had published her best-sellers. Perhaps the tarnish of stark reality is what we avoid when seeking to be diverted with a story, the bones must have fact, the flesh may be as chimeric as the reader can stand, his choice of reading being his latent utopian dream. Those with a highly developed sense of imagination are able to accept Ethel's divine afflati for what they are, and return with two feet set firmly on the ground. It is those who cannot trust themselves to return safely who cannot take her romances. Ethel had a finely developed sense of humour, that accounted for her ability to jump from romance to the intentionally ridiculous and back again with such success. Naturally those who read and were temporarily carried away by her books, wanted to know what she looked like. One is bound to feel curious about the appearance of someone who can hold your attention so successfully.

Ethel did not withhold her image from the public in order deliberately to create a mystery; she genuinely disliked the look of her own face, and no nun could have taken less trouble to adorn her own body. Her nature was reclusive and intensely private, never more so than after marriage, when interference by publicity could have wrecked a critical moment in her and Gerald's lives, possibly affecting both her peace and productivity.

Ethel was fully aware that she had her critics in the press, and that nothing exasperated them more than constant use of clichés yet she made no attempt to weed them out. Conversation in the nineteen-twenties revolved inextricably round such expressions. No genuine attempt to portray ordinary contemporary speech could fail to use them. Once she makes a half apology; '"When money gets into the wrong hands it's the root of all evil". "I've no doubt", said Mr. Weeks, shaking his head with a vague wonder as to where he had heard that remark before.'

The whole *Passer-by* collection of loosely linked stories is aimed at excusing either her own attitude to publicity, or the fallacies of the Greater British Public, who wrote to her in their thousands, and to whom she owed so much. If it was a fallacy that all Americans had penetrating eyes, this was part of her faith in the common myth; if it was fascinating apparently to have Red Indian blood in one's veins, then why not make use of the idea? There is one story for the district nurse, another for the lady's maid, one for the gambler, and another for the reader shattered by war wounds but still carrying on a bare existence.

Without television, and with much less 'time off' than would be acceptable now, reading was of great importance to the domestically orientated worker who knew with what grateful relief she could relax in Ethel's romantic flights of fancy. Chapters were kept short enough to be read quickly. Ethel really thought she was writing for the public and not for herself. So did she consider herself crusading? Possibly, yes. No young girl who read one of Ethel's novels could possibly present herself for marriage except as a virgin. Virginity was the 'in' thing (much as free love is now), due in part, perhaps, to Ethel's popularity.

One wishes that Ethel had understood children's ages better; the ones she describes seem so precocious and to have been given adult reactions. Writing about a child of seven, she says, 'The Woman's love of romance was strong in her,' 'And did she love him?' she demanded keenly.' This may in part have been due to her infrequent contact with real children, and then only with myself—or Ella's Brat, as Gerald called me—who was treated as an adult, and had no siblings to rub off the forward edges.

That the highest accolade, that could in those days be awarded anyone, was to call him or her a brick, seems rather limiting. But apparently it was satisfying enough to its all too frequent recipients throughout Ethel's novels, the lack of variety in this form of praise underlining how unquestioningly it was accepted. Dense and roseate, a brick is a compound substance with which to build solid futures, perhaps, but in constant verbal usage then, and clearly Ethel saw nothing strange about it.

With a cross between Hiawathan eurythmics and parish magazine sentimentality, Ethel composed an introductory poem for each book. Perhaps the most quotable is the one facing the first page of *The Black Knight*, published in the following year, 1927.

The Crusader

He did not seek the battle,
　　As he did not shun the test;
He bore the shock of conflict
　　Unshaken, though hard-pressed,
For the shield in which he trusted
　　Was the Cross upon his breast.

And when the fight was over,
　　Triumphant o'er the rest,
Stood the knight of stainless honour,
　　Who had simply done his best,
And had placed his trust unflinching,
　　In the Cross upon his breast.

The 'Black Knight' is a strong silent hero with a headstrong young heroine called Ermine, who has an aunt named Minerva. There is an English titled family of Devereux descent, and a Hildebrand who was a Courtenaye. An intercontinental mixture of classical cum troubadour lineage, yet some of these people have synonyms such as 'The White Rabbit' and 'Sambo'. The whole scene is set in uppercrust English society.

'Ye Gods' is a favourite exclamation of consternation. Ella used frequently to appeal to the heavens in this way, whether because the dog had been sick in the car, a vital piece of internal elastic had snapped, or even on receipt of a particularly choice piece of gossip. But with or without the Gods, Ethel in her struggle to find new fields wherein to exercise her Vestal mind, seems in *The Black Knight*, to jettison common sense from most of the writing. A girl who apparently had done no more harm than be insolent, is called 'You infernal jade' by her brother-in-law, while it is apparently considered perfectly reasonable that a girl of twenty-two could be dismissed to her room, and not allowed to descend until given permission. There are tired re-births of exhausted plots, and almost demoniacal persistence with getting girls safely married off, with the rejected lover eventually winning the field. Ethel was beginning to feel the strain of preoccupation with perpetual passion, and it shows.

How difficult it must have been to keep up the youthful tension needed to inspire the re-creation of young love.

Ethel was now forty-seven, a tricky moment in any woman's life. She was not well, although it was to be another two years before she knew how ill she really was. This may be why her little fetishes are less well disguised and her passion for red-gold hair and amber eyes with a green glint is given full rein in the heroine who spends much time brushing or shaking her hair about her shoulders, and flashing her eyes. Perhaps subconsciously she was churning out the pedestrian parts and lingering longer where her own pleasures lay.

Whipping had come back after a pause of several books, and young women (not teenagers) lay on beds together talking and whispering in the dark, warm arms wrapped about each other, planting small kisses. Was she missing Ella as much as Ella was missing her?

With the newness of married life now worn off, did she regret her old secure home? Perhaps so when Gerald was in a particularly military mood, or was throwing his class about and offending his employees; he had not been called a strict disciplinarian for nothing by his commanding officer during the war. Of all her novels, perhaps this book jars most on the subject of upper-class preoccupations. No one seems to have a job, all their activities are directed towards pleasure, money drops as manna from the skies, young people own houses, rough shooting, horses, hounds, and can afford to belong to expensive clubs, eat at expensive restaurants, and go to Hunt Balls whenever they feel like it. It's all pure *Tatler*, her excuse for this background being her certainty that real goodness lies behind even those self-indulgent characters. Anything less Tatlerish than herself would be impossible to imagine, yet she did not moralise; for her, faith was enough.

Those who knew Ethel superficially said that she looked through your eyes right into your soul. If she did this with me I was unaware of it (being so shortsighted that I would not have known if she was looking at me at all), and feel rather relieved to have been spared what must surely have been a most discomforting experience. She certainly looked into the soul of Ermine, and put down all that she saw there.

The Casino at Valrosa is described as a den of the most evil wickedness, full of allurement and evil promise, where a fancy-dress Cardinal dressed in red gives Ermine a leering look. Shocking, of course, but this was just another way of conveying temptation, which continually absorbed Ethel's mind. Without temptation there would have been no reason to write. The triumph of good over evil, love over hate, these are the key-stones on which she built up her entire imagery.

Was Ethel a prude? Ermine wakes up on the morning after her engagement and says to herself 'I wonder if I shall ever sleep decently again'. The meaning of *decently* can be misconstrued. Then again, 'why do women put up with it?' she said. 'Why—why—why? To be slaves of desire and victims of all evil impulses—all the ungovernable animal in man. What fools—what fools! And then call it life.' One suspects that Gerald had a pretty thin time of it while she was in this mood, especially if, as usual, she was identifying with her heroine.

This in turn brings the question of suicide into uncomfortable prominence. Was Ethel suicidal? She describes an attempt with great depth of feeling, 'A sort of frenzy of despair got hold of me, it was as if an iron door had shut on my only chance of escape. And then I heard an express—and I knew what I would do. It was like something dragging me. The next thing I knew, I was on the line, wondering how long it would take . . .'. This was the second time that she had described this feeling, the first having been in *Tetherstones*, the book written immediately after her marriage.

With Ethel's absurdities, her panting, her hard shivers, her faints, and her *dislike* of illicit love, there is so much deliberate over-writing here one wonders whether her sense of fun may not have come into its own. Was she intentionally pandering to her readers? Having no false hopes of going down to posterity as a great writer, could Ethel have been deliberately stressing the disparity between her own life and that of her characters in order to reveal herself as a flesh and blood woman, not just a pen, writing under direction from some celestial being?

Ethel's rather misleading descriptions of the South of France originated from Ella, who by now regularly wintered abroad. This was a move made advisable by an illness of mine, and one which Ella welcomed. It enabled her to let Blackmoor, and live there only during the summer. Ella did not share Ethel's horror of the fleshpots, her earlier trips to Switzerland having whetted her appetite for hotel life where gregarious collections of people gathered to have a good time, amply catered for by the management. A ball and at least two trips to the Casino every week, with a daily thé-dansant to while away dull afternoons—these were the gay times of which Ella's enthusiastic descriptions must have shocked Ethel and been the cause of her disapproval, so evident in *The Black Knight*. That I, too, should be exposed to all this, really horrified her, but had she known what a lovely time I was in fact having, at very little risk to my morals, she might have felt less anxious.

How hard Ethel worked may be gauged by the mere number of words which she published between October 1926 and the end of 1927. Having finished *The Black Knight*, a book of some 153,000 words, during 1926 she then completed the third volume of her 'Nick Ratcliffe Saga', called *By Request*, which added another 135,000.

SIXTEEN

Ethel Ill

By Request obviously gave her great pleasure to write. Her characters were old friends, deriving from her first and most famous novel *The Way of an Eagle.* Writing this third book in the series must have been like recounting a part of her own family life, so in harmony was she with her subject. Everyone in it reacts to each other in a predictable way which must have commended the book, particularly to her oldest fans. The feeling of family continuity was all the stronger because the time factor coincided with reality, so that Nick, created in 1912, was now perfectly right in his role as Great Uncle. The characters know all about each other and their antecedents, thus taking the reader both back in memory and forward in anticipation. It is with relief, however, that one observes how 'with it' the younger generation are, and that Ethel, immured in the country, with no radio (nor, of course, television), and with only newspapers and magazines to tell her about the outside world, had managed to catch the friable superficiality of the later nineteen-twenties so exactly. Their speech and mannerisms, habits and brittleness are all pointed up beautifully by the older generation to which she herself belonged. All three novels, *The Way of an Eagle, The Keeper of the Door,* and *By Request,* deal with people of her own standing.

Always extremely observant, noting both physical aberrations as well as thoroughly enjoying the 1920s' idea of beauty, Ethel wisely did not attempt anything profound; her writing was instinctive rather than studious, her characters are seldom clever or given to intellectual pursuits. Perhaps Will Musgrave the widower, who devotes his life to building viaducts and tunnels after his wife's death, is the nearest Ethel comes to describing intellectual dedication. Even then she shows him to be an eccentric who works incessantly to kill his lonely hours, rather

112

than as a man who enjoys what he is doing. She even lets his acquaintances call him 'insane, but not dangerous'.

That the appelation might fit herself, would have astounded her, with her lack of interest in her looks, her indifference to food and pleasure, and her demonic concentration on her daily output of words. Unlike Ethel who worked away in her room until she had completed her day's quota and would then come out, locking the door behind her, Gerald needed to show off what he had been up to. In this, he was not unlike Will Musgrave. Downstairs in his workshop Gerald drew plans, and made model railway stock which really worked, exquisitely wrought in steel and iron, which he finally delicately painted and polished. This workshop floor was sometimes ankle deep in steel filings, there was a smell of hot metal and engine oil, retorts for bending and angling were clamped to the benches while stacks of whippy steel sheeting lay against the walls, waiting to be moulded into intricate shapes.

Ethel's feelings about being frequently required to go and see how he was getting on are echoed in this passage in *By Request*:

> She had seen nothing of Chawalkhand so far since all father's interests were centred in the opposite direction . . . where his viaduct was in process of construction . . . this he had taken her to with pathetic enthusiasm to see, and she had in fact been warmly interested, but when it transpired that he planned as a matter of course that she should accompany him twice, if not thrice a day on his visits (up the valley) her ardour began to wane a little, she realised that much as she admired his work . . . she lacked the only thing which in her father's eyes was worth while, a brain of an engineer. She had begun to wonder anxiously how soon he would discover it, and be disappointed for she was too essentially honest to assume an attitude which she did not possess!

This is so Ethelian; she could not dissemble neither could she tell a lie.

Friendship between women was always of great importance to Ethel, and was reflected in this passage from the same book:

> 'Is the gift of childhood ever given to a woman?' There was pathos in the words . . . as went straight to the warm deeps

of Peggy's heart, she suddenly wished that Noel would go
away and leave them alone together—to make friends.

And a few sentences farther on:

'There is no such thing as time for those who are happy' said
Mrs. Forbes in her slow fatalistic fashion. 'For others there
is nothing else.'

Is Ethel perhaps here telling us that, busy as she is, she
herself is not happy?

Throughout this nostalgic book, 'Home' means England, and
is faithfully spelt with a capital, whereas 'home' means only
one's family place. It had been the same in *The Way of an Eagle*
and again in *The Keeper of the Door*, thus spanning twenty years
without change. Although the expression was widely in use
overseas until the early sixties, it seems to have been Ethel who
gave it the capital. Her works, like those of Kipling, were to be
found in all club libraries, from India throughout the far-flung
Empire; not only did she amuse the less well-to-do classes, she
was read by bored colonial wives, as they lay sweating on their
charpoys during afternoon siesta. Her influence must have been
considerable, giving many of the less imaginative women some
strangely alien ideas to think about. Particularly those to whom
church-going was almost entirely a social gathering where
dresses would be shown off and eyes exchange messages. That
any real or moral good could come from visiting a church must
to them have been a novel idea. Even as trysting-places, Ethel's
churches could cast a cloak of respectability.

How does Ethel understand this business of falling in love?
She makes an old flame of Nick Ratcliffe, hero of *The Way of an
Eagle*, say 'I'd give something to see him again, he was the
jolliest man I ever met', to which her husband replies, 'Every
woman who met Nick *wanted* to fall in love with him, but
luckily for him he had a genius for avoiding complications, which
is not given to many.' Does Ethel imply that the ideal man has
the power to switch a woman on at will, and that he does not
use this ability unless he means to go through with it and marry
her? Ethel certainly felt that the strong guiding hand in any
matter of the heart must be masculine, and that female encouragement was to be written off as intrigue. Consider her own

marriage. Ethel was ready to fall in love with Gerald, but, aided by Norah, he tipped the balance. Together they were weightier than Ella.

Ethel liked to think that woman was a pawn. Occasionally she might be allowed a little leeway, but that a woman should make all the running, Ethel would at that time have considered un-thinkable—worse still, unladylike.

Ethel was a natural breadwinner; she devoted herself to work because she loved it. She knew it gave widespread pleasure, the rewards were incidental and were to be returned whence they came. Once Gerald had been comfortably provided for and their establishment had risen to what was then known as an upper middle class household, she made over all her earnings to distressed gentlefolk and the societies which catered for them. That her own brother came under this heading was unfortunate, but just one more little cross to bear in the name of charity.

Reggie, never very strong-minded, had been made weaker by his bullying and drunken wife, who maltreated their children to such an extent that Ella considered reporting her to the R.S.P.C.C. Reggie may have been weak, but he was no fool. Charming, sober, and with his cultivated Edwardian stutter, he used to turn up for lunch at Ewhurst, and could twist Ethel round the ribbon of his eyeglass. His thin figure would be dressed in the latest striped suit, but the effect of this and of the boater of cream straw which he wore on his head was sometimes impaired by a pair of white spats, which made him look vaguely like a beach entertainer on holiday. Having rung up the night before, to make sure of a good lunch, he would wait until Gerald returned to his workshop and then sit with Ethel all afternoon pouring out his troubles, eventually leaving with a nice fat cheque to tide him over until next time. He was far too astute to bring his family with him.

In the New Forest, Ella also had visits from her brother, but of a very different kind. He would arrive *en famille*, a collection of worried-looking children would tumble out of the car, followed by their mother whose first port of call would be the downstairs lavatory, where, according to Ella, she would quench her permanent thirst from a hip flask.

The children, too timid to play, would wander unhappily round the garden, and look nervously at the horses over the hedge. Their pale pinched faces flinched if their mother put out an arm to keep the youngest off the flower beds. I could not understand it at all, and felt sad and most discomforted. I was used to jolly, affluent children to play with, and could not understand why they should be so frightened of animals, and poorly dressed. I did not find out the reason for many years to come. Meanwhile Ella would take Reggie into the study, a small room off the front door, and deal with him promptly. Her idea was to get them quickly on the move again, preferably before they could get into the drawing room and sit on the magenta silk chair covers, or worse put sticky fingers on the grand piano, an instrument which Ethel had had especially made for her.

Reggie played his cards remarkably well, and managed to extract a fair sum of money from his two sisters, each thinking that he came only to her. If either had known he was 'touching' the other, both sources would have stopped immediately. He had a job, but the 'extras' he received from his sisters helped him to pursue his bibulous habits—'extras' that were supposed to go for the children's clothes and food, his youngest child in 1928 being about three years old. What Reggie did with his portion of Ethel's settlement was always a mystery; £30,000 had disappeared, and was never recovered.

Ella, however, was busy doubling her share. During those long summers of the late twenties when the sun shone more hours than at any time until 1976, Ella made the most of her beautiful surroundings. The library had been opened out on to a loggia, and there, beneath the overhanging curtain of wisteria, breakfast was taken every morning, her loved Granny Parrott's silver shining in the sunlight. Her guests were enchanted with the atmosphere of gracious good living. Many of her friends from Guildford came to stay, also Maurice Bowra and his brother Edward, now firmly established young men, Edward in the army, and Maurice at Oxford, both to do as well as Ella had predicted all those years ago when she had taught them their first lessons at Knockholt. Ella gathered a scholarly, talented group of people around her, most of them younger than herself, who delighted in her amusing repartee, and enjoyed listening to her playing and singing after dinner. This was perhaps the happiest part of her life.

Like most pleasant interludes, it came to an end unexpectedly.

Accustomed to being given large presents by Ethel, Ella continued to spend lavishly, but a jealous Gerald suddenly put his foot down. Ella had been given her lot and she should make do with it. Ella tossed her head and said that it would make not the slightest difference if Ethel never gave her another penny. Then with alacrity she put Blackmoor on the market, found a boarding school for me to attend during the summer, and packed away all her precious possessions until she could house them again. This was the beginning of the hard frost between Gerald and Ella. Until then they had been barely polite to each other; afterwards both went to great lengths to avoid meeting. It must have distressed Ethel greatly.

Making her headquarters at Durrants Hotel, Manchester Square, Ella took a suite, and hired a piano from Harrods. She hated London, but it was the most sensible place to be in order to keep up with her friends while she had no house in which to entertain them. The summer before she had found a delightful wild part of Dorset, on the far side of Poole Harbour. When it was time to take me back from school for the holidays, she left London, collected Patsy, and with great enthusiasm bought a horse-drawn caravan in Ringwood, and we three set out from there to clop our way to Dorset, Ella dressed for the part in gipsy clothes and dangling gold hoop earrings. The caravan was heavy, the horse, Captain, was lazy, at every hill he stopped, and Patsy had to go off in the pony trap, to fetch another horse to help him up to the top. Nothing however was going to mar the fun for Ella. She had provided a black cat, and a canary in a cage, I was put into shorts and had a scarf tied round my head, and found, to my great surprise, that Ella could cook well.

This was to be the first of a series of heavenly summers spent going back to nature, every bit as enjoyable as the sophisticated winters we continued to spend in the Riviera. Eventually Ella put up a long wooden building on the site of our first camping ground, and it was still there at the beginning of the 1939 War. We called it the Hut, and because of the unconventional atmosphere there Ella was unlikely to be bothered with visits from her brother-in-law. Gerald disliked anything that was not totally conventional and correct, and Ethel, being the dutiful wife she was, bowed to her husband's preferences. Ella and Ethel continued to write to each other frequently, and when Ella was in

London they had long telephone conversations held, I am sure, when Gerald was away playing boats with Tom.

Every winter we occupied the same suite of rooms in the Riviera Palace Hotel, Menton, that we had used continually since my fifth birthday. We were habituées there, and the staff were known friends who welcomed us back year after year, looking after my budgerigars, and a marmoset until our unfailing return in the autumn.

I was sent to the English School in Menton, which was full of many nationalities, and to a dancing school also attended by Prince Rainier of Monaco. We were of an age, he was a rather nice plump boy.

Between 1926 and 1929, Ethel had been slowly becoming a sick woman. By 1927 she was writing less regularly, and becoming over-tired very easily. A book which she published in that year shows her at her most primitive. On reading the four stories contained in *The House of Happiness*, one is tempted to think that they must have been dredged up from her youth and been only slightly polished before being presented to her faithful public. Cassell, who published them, certainly took a risk, yet they also went into a second edition by 1930. Reading them more carefully I am almost certain that they were in fact new work ground out under the influence of pain-killing drugs. The framework of the stories is there but the action and dialogue are so clipped one can scarcely recognise them as being Ethel's. Yet the situations and reactions are too mature to have been early work. There is not a light moment in any of them, and her sense of humour is completely lacking; obviously she was pushing herself to get the work done.

Some of this strain must have become obvious to Ella, who persuaded Ethel that she would benefit from a few months in the sunshine, telling her of a pleasant hotel near Cap Ferrat. Gerald agreed that it would do her good provided that Ella and I were out of the way by the time they arrived. This was easily accomplished as we were in the habit of returning in a leisurely fashion to England via the Italian Lakes, staying at Menaggio and going to see the azaleas in the gardens of the Villa Carlotta.

Three months in the warm spring sunshine on the Riviera certainly did Ethel good, but as an exercise in pleasure it was a disaster. She loathed every minute, she felt alien, she disap-

proved of the other English residents, and was deeply shocked
by the apparent superficiality of the life on the Côte d'Azur. It is
doubtful if she went far outside the gates of the hotel. Gerald
would have supported her in her dislike, anything un-English
was to him unspeakably taboo. That French people should have a
right to be French on their own soil would never have occurred to
him; one can imagine how unpopular he must have made himself.

Ella and I spoke French easily, another mark against us. It
was indeed a good thing that we were not in the vicinity, as I can
imagine how affronted Ella would have felt.

From an author's angle, however, the trip was not totally
wasted. Ethel managed to get a book out of her experiences,
which she wrote some years later, but her immediate reaction
on her return to England was to write *The Gate Marked Private*.

There is no dedication or verse to introduce the right atmo-
phere of this book or give the reader any inkling of what is inside.
This suggests that the book's meaning will be obvious to anyone
concerned. Ethel would never reveal or identify by implication,
lest she cause distress; her concern was to protect her sources by
the circuitous anonymity of her tale. That she thought it right
and proper to tell this story may well mean that she felt she
could well be writing her last novel.

With an agricultural country setting, Ethel's thirtieth book
gets into the atmosphere of an English farming community,
which holds in its midst a man better bred than most, who
eventually marries a woman of even finer breeding than his own.
In all this they are aided, teased and finally irritated by the
woman's niece, who when no one suspects such a possibility
elopes with a member of the local aristocracy.

Ethel's mind was happy, slogging along English muddy
lanes; her pen here records her love of the countryside as well as
in any novel she had written. She was thankfully shaking off
France, and revelling in English eccentricities and in the hard
struggle of farming, about which she proved to be remarkably
knowledgeable. Yet Ethel was aware how seriously ill she was,
and her weakness is mentioned many times. She describes over-
tiredness:

It was not sleep that came upon her, but a kind of stupor
through which she was aware of that curious unevenness of

heartbeats and a strange sense of oppression that seemed to develop therefrom. But at length, gradually, the burden began to lift, and she raised her head with a guilty feeling of having suffered herself to give way. Wearily she got up from her lowly seat, but the next moment she reeled dizzily with closed eyes against the whitewashed wall. Her brain seemed to have turned fluid and she could not steady it. . . . With supreme effort she gathered up the reins of her self-control. This was absurd. She took herself seriously to task. There was nothing the matter, save that she was a trifle over-tired.

Yet the book is full of life, and her humour is back again, chipping through the medium of the adolescent girl. Whatever else Ethel had, she possessed courage. Perhaps the most poignant passage in the book is where the young girl discovers that the woman she had always believed to be her aunt is really her mother. All the family except the niece knew, and she feels that she has been shut out and deceived. Her reaction is to elope with a most unsuitable and elderly, albeit aristocratic roué.

Ethel, still far from well, was persuaded by both Gerald and Ella to go and see a specialist in Winchester, recommended by Norah. What he saw put her straight into hospital, and within twenty-four hours her right breast had been removed. How long she had hidden the lump no one knew, it would have been typical of her to have said nothing for as long as possible, hiding her pain and discomfort so as not to worry Gerald. There is also an element of shyness here, it would have been very distressing for her to have to admit pain in what was to Ethel such a private place. She still dressed in longish clothes, wore thick stockings, and placed lace fichus in strategic places to hide any suspicion of a cleavage. I was at boarding school when the operation happened, but Ella kept me informed. It was clear that she was suffering nearly as much as Ethel herself, out of sympathy, and wringing out her heart in jealousy of Gerald who would not let her see Ethel, saying that she would excite her too much. Yet Norah, Gerald's sister, paid daily visits, and kept house for him while she was in hospital. It has been said that Norah could direct Gerald to do anything she wished, and this may absolve Gerald from any cruelty to Ella.

As soon as Ethel was home again, Ella rushed over to see

her, taking a pot of azaleas. These flowers seemed to have a magical significance for the sisters, as Ethel, too, would always choose them when she visited Ella. When she was expected, Ella would laughingly say to me, 'I wonder what colour she will bring this time?' The species was taken for granted. What Ella found when she was shown into Ethel's bedroom shocked her beyond belief. Ethel had lost so much weight, her face was sunken, and her hair, parted in the middle and drawn over her ears, had gone grey overnight. Her hands, normally white and elegant, were transparent with blue veins throbbing under the taut skin. Yet when Ella came in she sat up, and flung her arms out, making some joke about looking like a scarecrow. Even her voice, normally soft, was a harsh whisper, the sound coming and going with the shortness of her breath. Ella held her in her arms, fighting back the tears, tears which threatened to choke her as she tried hard to say something jolly and comforting. She felt sure she was in the presence of a woman who would not be on earth much longer.

Ethel, however, was not to be put down just yet. It took her many months to recover, but her writing did not falter. As soon as she was fit enough to do without a nurse, her daily routine of work began again, an hour or so at a time, until she was right up to her usual output. Norah, who lived in Guildford, found Ethel and Gerald a house in Winchester itself, which she pointed out would be better for Ethel than being right out in the country as she had been. Gerald agreed and drove Ethel over to have a look at the house. She did not much like it—a large, dark, Victorian mansion set into the side of a hill—but the advantages were obvious, so with great reluctance they moved there. Norah gave them much well-meaning assistance. She was delighted to have Gerald close, and could pop in and keep an eye on things herself now that 'darling' Ethel was so delicate.

SEVENTEEN

Ella Ill

ST. MARY'S SLEEPERS HILL was their home from 1930. It lay back from a steep road, hidden in high shrubs and trees, which gave the house a dank air. The over-ornate woodwork, painted a dreary dark green, reached out into the drive like a fussy hollow tentacle, ready to swallow the caller in the porch long before he could enter the gloomy hall tiled in brown and white, cold to the feet and menacing with its displays of Indian swords arranged in rosettes on the brown walls. The stairs rose in slippery polished stages, and it was not until one reached the drawing room door, usually slightly ajar, that one's feeling of safety returned. This is how I felt about visiting the house, and others tell me that they, too, remember it as a distinctly creepy building.

Ethel had made the house as cheerful as she was capable of doing, which meant using the same large dark furniture but indulging in nice new blue covers for the chairs, and a pink carpet. Her colour sense was never her strongest attribute, and Ella often laughingly told her she was colour blind; certainly she never seemed to enjoy describing the colours of clothes, and most of her characters have either blue or green eyes, and red, corn or black hair. The dining room was filled by a large highly polished table, covered with nice silver for meals, or stark naked between times; no one went in there except to eat, there was no point in putting flowers on the table. Coming out of this room you could either turn right and enter the drawing room, where coffee would be served, or left and through green baize doors into the kitchen whence were wafted smells far nicer than could possibly have come from the food that had just been eaten. That heavy brass-studded baize door held a fascination for me, its very squoosh as it swung to and fro was comforting, and the highly polished finger plate shone with hope.

The garden was on a steep slope, which made it unsuitable for Gerald's model railway, a great disappointment which he quickly overcame by switching to making model boats, with and without engines.

Storm Drift was written while recovering from the illness and published the year that she moved to Winchester. It could be called the poor relation of *By Request*, being the tortuous but eventually successful love affair of a rejected lover from that book. Ethel's Elysian lyricism was petering out, partly due to the effort of trying to adapt herself to the fast pace of the early 30's and also, perhaps, to a running-down of passion itself. She had had a late awakening to fact, and was now attempting to replenish the drained well with a wet mushiness. She is sentimental, oh yes; but can still wring a tear from the most sceptical and hardhearted reader, to his intense annoyance.

Storm Drift relies on an intimate knowledge of illness, and includes ill and dying people. Sickness was very much on her mind, her own life had so recently tottered on the edge of oblivion. She now wrote with a natural feeling, whereas previously her knowledge had been secondhand. To Ethel nothing in life was more important than affairs of the heart, yet more then ever they had to be directed by God and the participants were answerable to Him. Ethel saw her role as a medium between God and his people, and hoped his influence would be recognised in her writing. There is no suspicion of a tongue in her cheek, she spoke from the heart, and cared greatly that her characters should resolve their difficulties in a Godly way. Considering the conventions of the day, she is anything but a prude, nor does she proselytise, her little references to God and prayer are woven in perfectly naturally.

Ethel proposes some original ideas about suicide: 'We've really no right to go without invitation, I suppose it's trespassing,'—which makes one wonder how often she considered it for herself. Depression after serious illness and surgical shock can do odd things to the mind. I get the feeling that she would have done such a thing had it been for the good of someone else: that she did not, was not for lack of courage.

There is also a Divine humour, she likens her hero to the Image of God, but makes him kind, dumpy, unimaginative, and relatively inarticulate, a slightly ludicrous figure, and then with scorn matches him to an erstwhile 'go-go' dancer who repents so heartily that she doesn't want to go on living, truly a poor thing to be pitied. Although quivering smiles still persist, her own were usually to hide an inner desire to laugh, checked to spare hurt feelings. Descriptions of men cramming on hats to go paddling, or refraining from smoking in case a loved one should be dying, are almost certainly examples of cultural homilies, pointed out for fun. Tiggie the hero heaves about in the sea like a hippo, but inspires his wife to see him as a vision of glory.

Perhaps in *Storm Drift* she catches the sense of human physical awareness better than before, of tiny, detailed sensations that cannot be portrayed by screen or drama. Her own sensitivity to the feel of a hand, and the slight movement in response proves her a master of the immediacy of touch. Her writing could be said by now to have developed its own extra-sensory perception.

Soon after Ethel had recovered from her illness and while she was at work on *Storm Drift*, Ella came to the conclusion that she had drifted about without a home long enough, and that I should be sent regularly to boarding school. Ella's 'ship had come in', as she put it. Money she had invested after the sale of Blackmoor had by now doubled and she could contemplate building a house to suit our needs. A very pleasant parcel of land was found at Nutley in Sussex. Uncle John Dell, the ageing architect of the family, who lived in Bournemouth, was roped in to design the house, and Uncle Will, by now living with another sister in Boscombe (Aunt May having died), was asked to keep an eye on his elder brother and see that he did not over-spend.

Ella was expert at this sort of manipulation, keeping two crotchety old men busy and happily in touch with each other, while at the same time appearing to save herself the expense of an architect and surveyor. The result was an extremely pleasant, solidly-built house, no corners cut, the very building of which gave pleasure all round. Ella was extremely generous and although there were no actual fees, both Uncles John and Will were far better off after their co-operation. While *Storm Drift* was being written, Rest Harrow was being built. In the spring of 1930, as the book was being published, Ella was choosing curtain materials in London, and by July, Violet Ebsworth,

Ethel's beloved friend and personal secretary, was helping Ella with the final arrangements before the furniture arrived from storage in Southampton.

Ella had taken a cottage in the district while the house was being built and I had spent my holidays with her. It was an extremely exciting time, as I was consulted about what I would like, and how it was all to be planned. Not many girls of eleven or twelve are so blessed.

By the time that Ella and I were settled in Nutley, Ethel and Gerald had been resident at Winchester for about six months, and we began to see much more of Ethel than before. Obviously she loved Rest Harrow, which was indeed much nicer than St. Mary's. Gerald came too, but usually made some excuse to go off with Tom as soon as lunch was over.

There was a pause of yet another year before Ethel had another book published. Her environment was hardly cheerful, and once she made a start, Ella suddenly became seriously ill. Putting all work aside, she came over to Nutley immediately. Ella had double mastoid, nasty at the best of times, but made even more tricky as Ethel did not want her to go into hospital. Instead she had the house turned into a clinic, with the very best specialist and surgeon to operate, and three nurses. I was at home for the holidays, frantic with worry, trying my best to run things as they should be, but at that age it was not easy. It was also the first time in my life that a man had slept in the same house with us, I was fascinated to see socks hanging from the bottom of the bed rail, and pyjamas laid out at night. The cook and gardener were marvellous, but the worry of it all sent me to a nursing home in Hove with a burst appendix, so while Ethel and Gerald took over Rest Harrow, I was visited by Edith de Wolf, who lived close by, their old school friend from the 'Snobbery' Shrubbery in Streatham.

Ella very nearly died. Even with her three nurses and all the expertise that money could buy, the risk of operating in her bedroom had been almost too great, and an infection developed. She hovered between life and death for several days, then one evening the nurse left her bedroom door open and she heard Gerald talking to Ethel about sending me to a children's home. That rallied her fighting spirit and she began to pull through. By the time I got home, she was just out of danger. Ethel and

Gerald did not want to be involved at all with me and went home as soon as I got back.

Ella made a slow recovery and as I was not feeling too strong myself, we had a very quiet summer. Ethel would ring up every week to see that Ella was all right, and they talked for an hour at a time. The fact that both sisters had been so dangerously ill re-awakened their knowledge of how much they cared for each other; adversity had brought them closer together again than at any time since Ethel's marriage.

Ella had a greenhouse built at Rest Harrow, which became her greatest joy. She treated the plants like children, worrying if the sun was too hot, or the wind too cold, trotting backwards and forwards several times a day to see that all was well with them. Every evening she spent at least an hour watering and re-arranging and potting. Now the Georgian winecoolers were continually full of flowers of her own growing, and as I was away at boarding school so much of the time, the flowers gave her something to fuss over. This discovery of her green fingers did something to Ella's character; she grew much more mature, tried hard to keep her fits of jealousy over friends to herself where possible, and took to wearing clothes which were quieter and smarter, in fact becoming an easier person altogether. She once said to me 'Illness refines', and certainly she and Ethel were far less prickly in each other's company.

Soon Ethel began to come over for the day regularly, perhaps once a fortnight, leaving Gerald behind. Tom would drive her over in the Daimler. Ella was beside herself with pleasure at seeing Ethel so often, telling me how happy she was to renew the bond of friendship. She forgot that Ethel really did love Gerald. Perhaps she did not want to know, or even subconsciously wanted to drive a wedge between them by telling Ethel how much more like her old self she was becoming, provided that Gerald kept out of the way.

There were many reasons why Gerald should choose to stay behind; he disliked listening to women talking, he disliked both Ella and me, and above all things he disliked Rest Harrow . . . for the very reason that Ethel liked it, it was so much nicer than St. Mary's. Ella, whom he had hoped was a 'goner', had risen from the ashes mightier than before, and must now for the first time have seemed a definite threat to him.

I watched Ethel during those all-day visits. She wandered round the garden arm-in-arm with Ella, talking incessantly. Two tall women taking long slow strides together, pausing every now and then to examine a plant, or conclude a discussion. Ella, being taller, would hold Ethel at arm's length now and then to see her expression, or tuck her arm even closer with a laugh and a squeeze. They both had large feet, Ella in particular, and the same determined way of putting down their heels first, then gradually taking the weight on to the rest of the foot.

Ella, who was enjoying taking time to recover, would go off and rest in her sunparlour after lunch, leaving Ethel to wander off down to the wood, taking the dogs with her. At that time we had two; Jess, a delicate, nervous collie, and Rags, my white West Highland terrier, who liked being taught tricks. The private wood, one of the delights of Rest Harrow, had a stream flowing through it which at one point opened out into a still pond. Ethel loved being able to wander there undisturbed. Around four o'clock I would go and bring her back for tea. She could usually be found on a bench that overlooked the pond, her hands in her lap, sitting slightly forward, her hat squarely on her head, and a scarf round her shoulders. She would see me and rise with a wistful smile, accept my arm and allow herself to be led up the hill again. Ethel did not talk much, unless she had seen some wild thing she wanted to identify. She thought me shockingly forward, far too much of a woman of the world for my thirteen years, and regretted this.

Tom maintained their old Daimler, the same car that had taken Ethel and Gerald on their honeymoon ten years previously, in a pristine condition. The upholstery was in grey cord to match Lady Jane's exterior, the cream pull-down blinds had silk tassels, and the speaking tube hung coiled on the window strut, shining and ready to hand. Ethel's fur rug lay folded on the seat, a footwarmer ready on the floor. I would get in and try out all the gadgets, and be shown how the heavy plate glass windows rose or fell at the touch of a button. Tom thoroughly enjoyed having a young person to show off to. In this very car I had been appallingly sick on my way to have my appendix out. I was mortified and begged Tom to forgive me. He was so nice and said, 'You forget about it Miss Poppy, we all have our troubles from time to time'. That he looked forward to these visits was obvious, our own staff welcomed him enthusiastically and were full of questions about Ethel and her ways. Tom would remain loyally mysterious, and happily important.

One unfortunate day Ethel told Ella that Gerald had not been very fit, his leg had been playing him up again. Ella at once put it down to gout, and hinted that such an ailment was caused by drink. Ethel was astonished, summoned Tom from the servant's sitting room, and returned to Winchester before tea, making some polite excuse. Ethel was never rude, she withered into silence and looked hurt, knowing how much more upsetting it could be.

It was the end of the summer and time for me to go back to school. Letters from Ella did not mention Ethel so frequently, they had started to release themselves from the close bond that had been woven after each had been so ill. Both were now as fit as could be expected, Ethel was anxious to take up her pen again, Ella to renew her pattern of visits from friends. Carefully dovetailed invitations were sent, with no overlapping, so that the very best could be got out of each minute. Ella was a demanding friend, but a delightful companion. She was also a fund of information, some of it bizarre, as when she told Mary Bastard, by now a very dried-up spinster, that the reason why she had so much magenta in the drawing room was its well-known and delicious effect on the passions. Poor Mary blushed in speechless agony, testifying to Ella's theory. Another large and well-built female friend remembers her own amusement and discomfiture, when she called out to Ella, who was marching ahead of her on a very hot and steep climb up the downs, 'I'm not far behind, Ella darling, following you with little hot pants', to which Ella replied, 'Not so little, I think'. When Ella laughed all the world heard, a melodious contralto shout of delight.

Remembering Ethel as she was then, quiet, refined, breathing her laughter through a slightly downy mouth, never raising her voice, or gesticulating with her hands, it is hard to reconcile this repressed image, with the Ethel who wrote this passage from a short story called *The Chatelaine* in 1931.

'I can't do it!' she cried to him. 'I can't go!'
'Why not?' he said.

She answered him between tears and laughter. 'I—I don't know. I don't know. I think—it's because—though you are such a brute—I love you!'

'My darling!' he said, and in that instant she was in his arms, held fast—beyond all hope of escape, while he kissed her closely, passionately, as no man had ever kissed her before.

When he curbed himself at length he saw that her eyes were wet, 'I've hurt you,' he said with compunction. 'Oh Chatelaine forgive me! I'm a brute!'

She laughed in answer—the soft mocking laughter with which many a woman hides a soul.

'Yes, yes, you are a brute,' she said, 'But never mind! Do it again!'

Was Ethel baring her soul, or was she mocking? How can people, less than fifty years ago, have accepted *The Chatelaine*? No self-respecting writer could weather the ridicule such prose would produce today, yet the vast majority of Ethel's readers swallowed it whole, making no complaints. Most of the reviewers had by now given up.

A friend of Ella's who met Ethel unexpectedly at Rest Harrow told her that she considered her writing beautiful. Ethel blushed faintly and said 'That's very kind of you, and most undeserved, they are not well written and will never be called classics'. She appeared very pleased however with the 'pretty compliment', and gave a gracious smile.

In those days, annoyance was often expressed physically, rather than verbally, frequently by stamping. Not only children stamped their feet in impatience but grown men stamped in fury, sometimes flinging walking-sticks over hedges in their annoyance. Emotional manifestations of this sort occur in Ethel's writing, and they certainly happened with Ella, who was quite capable of pulling off a glove and casting it at the foot of someone who dared to challenge her authority. After the astonished offending party had slunk away she would pick up her glove, put it on again, humming a little tune, a dark light of triumph in her blue-black eyes. Ella's attitude to life was very similar to that of the Chatelaine, autocratic and domineering, yet that last scene of passion would never have been laid at Ella's door. That Ethel's passion scenes so often verge on the ridiculous shows she was weakest where she had least personal knowledge. Gerald's great joy in Ethel was her sweetness and gentility, had he forced her to accept unbridled passion he would have lost the very thing for which he married her. Besides, unbridled passion is not a one-sided affair, as Ethel herself continually points out. Except out of frustration Gerald was unlikely to ever have felt greatly roused. Playing boats with Tom was evidently sufficient excitement, seeming to underline the adage that the nicest men never grow up.

Loyalty was Ella's strongest attribute. No matter what she was doing, if one of her many woman friends was in trouble she would fly to her assistance, taking over the household and directing the recovery, much to the astonishment and sometimes annoyance of any family. She was also capable of interfering if she thought a child or adolescent was not getting proper tuition.

Ella would interfere outrageously over educational problems, and give gratuitous advice that cost her several older friends and gained her new young ones. Where Ethel was preoccupied with the adult problem Ella was fascinated with that of youth. She had no compunction about turning children against their parents, if she thought it would be for their good. Both sisters were visionary; one actively, the other passively.

EIGHTEEN

No Public Image

ETHEL WROTE more books at St. Mary's than at any other
house she ever lived in. Evidently the dull quietness of the place
suited her temperament. *The Prison Wall*, a tale of a well-
brought up young man in search of his ex-convict father and his
loves and misjudgements en route, is what would at the time
have been called a 'nice' book, very evocative of its period.
Australia is seen as a promising young country out to challenge
the world and forget its convict forebears. The scenery is
different, but Ethel's easily predictable emotional reactions
remain constant. The Australian accent, attitude and ambigu-
ousness are very well described. In almost every book of Ethel's
there is one line that, even in its correct context, is totally
baffling. *The Prison Wall* is no exception. Here it is, flourishing
what hidden meaning? *'I will only make love to you with your feet
on my neck.'* No doubt to Ethel the sense was transparently clear,
but the visual image is, to say the least, contorted.

The Silver Wedding, brought out in 1932, has, I fear, a portrait of myself in it; a tiresome thirteen-year-old who is bright
and offhand with grown-ups, and much disliked by middle-aged
men. Goldie is a little beast, and undoubtedly a Brat as well.
Erich Morven's attitude to her is identical with Gerald's to
myself; cheerfully reciprocated.

There are many items of everyday living that Ethel never
mentions with any interest in her books. Food is one of them,
perhaps because her own eating habits were so puritan and
tasteless. She would have regarded it as self-indulgent and a sin
to enjoy her food. All the same, she did allow herself a few
quirks of taste. She had a passion for small jelly biscuits covered
in chocolate, which were quite a rarity, seldom coming more
than two to a tin of 'teatime mixed'. At four o'clock a selection
of these would be put on a plate and brought in on the swing
cake stand. If there were no 'little round jelly ones' she would be

quite aggrieved, having secretly been looking forward to them all the afternoon. A lunch favourite was whiting baked with its tail in its mouth and smothered in Heinz tomato sauce served from a silver jug. This would often be followed by hot chocolate semolina pudding, drowned again, but this time in tinned cream. Breakfast, however, was of the sort traditionally approved on Sundays, yet Ethel had it every day. London haddock topped with a poached egg was what she needed, having already done three or four hours' work in the early morning. None of these was fare to inspire the best from her domestics, but on days when the family came to lunch, cook was allowed to break out and be more inventive. The cook was left to concoct her own menus; Ethel would then go over them with her, stifling an occasional yawn as she did so.

The cook, Jean, was a diminutive twenty-year-old who looked even younger and had added a few years to her age when she came to Ethel. She was devoted, having been more or less rescued by Ethel from a post where she had been very unhappy. Seeing her letter to the servants' agency to which Jean had applied for another job, Ethel ignored the conventions, swept to the house where she had been working, found her employers were out for the day and engaged her on the spot.

Always a disciplinarian with herself, if not with others, Ethel adhered to a strict regimen which was to continue throughout her life. She was called every morning at seven o'clock, breakfasted downstairs with Gerald at eight and then, after sorting out which of her letters should be answered that afternoon and which left for her beloved Violet Ebsworth to deal with next time she came down, she would have her morning discussion with Jean, arrange the flowers and, promptly at ten o'clock, be ready to go out for the morning.

If it was fine, she would put on her walking shoes and carry a stick, going off into the woods quite on her own, no note book or book to read, just a coat and scarf if it was chilly, and always a wide-brimmed hat, felt in winter, straw in the summer. If it was wet or too cold, Tom would take her out in the car. Wrapped up well with rugs and a cushion, she held the speaking tube in her hand and told Tom to slow down whenever she saw anything to interest her. The Packard that she had at that time had special blinds so that if she did not wish to be seen she could draw them very quickly, and sit back in privacy. Tom had no discussions with her on these trips, and according to the staff Ethel 'did her meditating' then, or when out walking; she was virtually alone, the glass panel between the chauffeur and herself ensuring complete privacy. In the woods no one knew where she went, and it would have been unthinkable to follow her.

By twelve-thirty she would be back and getting ready for lunch. Afterwards she would inform the parlourmaid if she was 'at home' or 'not at home'. 'At home' usually meant that she was expecting someone by appointment, but 'not at home' that she could relax, answer letters or knit until tea time knowing that she would not be disturbed. Knitting was of great importance to her at that time, she knitted all her own dresses, skirts and cardigans, mostly in blue-grey heather mixture on fine needles. Evidently the repetitive movement was soothing and she could think about her current book at the same time. Beside her would be her old attaché case holding whatever manuscript she was currently working on, but she would seldom open it during the day. Ethel's intense shyness and self-effacing habits may have accounted for the need to make her own clothes, especially after a mastectomy. It would have been embarrassing for her to go and try on garments in a shop, or even have a dressmaker to the house. So with admirable economy, she carefully knitted the pieces, and then sent them away to be taped, and made up to fit. Her earnings at the time were still in the region of £30,000 a year, sometimes more.

In the evenings she and Gerald would listen to the radio, especially the six o'clock news. This was the only time of day in which they were together long enough to talk to each other, small talk that is forgotten as soon as spoken, friendly and inconsequential. Gerald would have a whisky and soda, or just soda, before they went upstairs to change for dinner, Gerald changing from a suit into velvet smoking jacket and dark trousers, Ethel into a short dress of the simplest style, always worn with the diamond brooch which Ella had given her as a wedding present. Dinner was served at seven fifteen. If they were alone, sitting at each end of a long table, it would be an almost silent meal, Ethel perfectly polite if spoken to but offering nothing to any conversation that Gerald might make. Sometimes Ethel would join Gerald in a little claret or chablis depending on the dish it was accompanying, and Gerald would occasionally have a glass of port with his cheese and biscuits.

After dinner coffee would be brought into the drawing room, Ethel would sip a little leaving most of it in her cup. As soon as she could decently do so Ethel would go to bed, feigning tiredness. By the time Gerald went upstairs to their room he would find his wife asleep in her single bed, her attaché case of manuscripts close beside her on the floor. He would have a bath, read a bit and then before long turn out the light.

As soon as Gerald was asleep, Ethel would silently steal out of bed, and taking the attaché case with her, go back to the bathroom. Here she had a warm carpeted room, an upright chair, a glass topped table and a good light. Locking the door she would settle down to write. Everyone else in the house was asleep, her own world of thoughts could crowd around her, keeping her the best company. Ethel was loyally left alone to fight her way across miles of foolscap paper—her big writing flowing over the page and becoming streamlined as her thoughts raced to be put down; the top of the page would still not be dry as she sped to the bottom and turned over. No one really knew how long she worked. Looking at her original manuscripts, one can see that she wrote unhesitatingly, rarely correcting herself except to alter an adjective or adjust a meaning on reading it through afterwards. Her dialogue seems to have been particularly speedily written, as if she could hear the conversation going on, and had difficulty keeping up with it.

Ethel's blue bathrooms both at St. Mary's and at Meadowlands, admittedly carpeted but otherwise strictly utilitarian, were the sole witness to whatever physical struggles she had. What pains she must have suffered when writing are not hard to imagine, a radical mastectomy removes much muscle, and the resultant scar draws the skin painfully when the arm is flexed. Yet she was never known to complain of pain, her fortitude was astonishing and part of her remarkable personality. Always far more interested in the happiness of her husband, friends and relations, she sublimated her own bodily failings, pains and desires.

Not until a tooth abscess became so unbearable that she was unable to sleep or stay still, but could only pace the house, would she consent to have a dentist to see her. When it was decided that the tooth must come out, their bedroom was turned into a surgery, her own doctor administered the anaesthetic, a nurse held her hand, and the dental surgeon removed the offending molar. She had insisted on locking the bedroom door, so Gerald was left to pace up and down outside on the landing, hands behind his back, backwards and forwards, frantic with worry and distress. The parlour maid told the cook that he looked like a man expecting his wife's first baby. 'That worked up he was.'

Ethel's horror of letting anyone see her in distress or pain was a very animal instinct to which she adhered right up to her last days. It caused her nearest ones as much agony as she was bearing herself, the very thing she wanted to avoid.

Over at Rest Harrow, Ella had had her eight tapestries made up into chair seats for the Hepplewhite chairs she had inherited from Granny Parrott. These complicated embroideries each representing a winter's work in the South of France, had been laboriously stitched, to while away dull mornings when the mistral was blowing and it was too unpleasant to venture outside. Ella could never sit about idly. Finishing each one had been a challenge to be completed before leaving for home.

Now that I was into my teens it seemed a good idea to build a tennis court and attract other people of my own age in the neighbourhood. A vast hole was excavated in the steep hillside beside the house with the detritus piled up at the sloping end. Ella was delighted and could immediately visualise the rock garden which she would have constructed over the mound of ugly earth. She now had plenty of scope for her horticultural talents. Old friends were constantly coming to stay, Nursie, Violet Ebsworth, Uncle Will Dell, Mary Bastard, and Edith de Wolf; the last two lived nearby on the coast, one at Worthing and one at Lancing. Cousin Eva Parrott's son, John Moxon, at school at Lancing, could be taken out for lunch, then Ella and I would go on for tea with Mary Bastard, who languished on into tired old age and depression, taking care of her mother, who lived to be 102.

Ethel kept up with Nursie mostly by letter. It was a difficult journey for her to make from Bromley, and hardly worth it just for the day. Ella and I saw much more of her. She would bring Peggy with her, now a tall lanky girl who had done extremely well at school and was training to be a pharmacist. The Hut which Ella had built on the original caravan site in Dorset continued to give immense pleasure, and for me it stands out as the most enchanted time of the holidays. A repeated dream to look forward to each summer, free from servants, and where one could let one's hair down. Rabbit-cropped grass sprang up under bare feet, there was riding, swimming, and walks across boggy moors where gentians and Dartford warblers were plentiful. A tidal creek full of marsh birds wound salty fingers round the base of the hill. Here a London family moored a houseboat, people who became welded into the pattern of our existence. Here, too, Ella entertained intimate friends, but Ethel never came, Gerald did not approve of any kind of hair-loosening, considering it a form of 'letting the side down', 'not playing the game'. All Ethel's heroes played the game so earnestly, how could he feel otherwise? Anyone who was not army was a 'damn civilian' in his ferocious estimation. Ethel by dint of marriage was considered within bounds, but Ella and I were irredeemably civilian *and* eccentric.

If Gerald read Ethel, one wonders what he made of all the trembling, fainting, panting and palpitations. For Ethel this would be a normal reaction to shock. Early risers, like herself, have (according to Dr. Marianne Frankenhaeuser) a much higher adrenalin level than other mortals. Ethel must have longed to behave like a rabbit and bolt every time she was startled. All the unused adrenalin coursing through her veins would cause trembling and dilated pupils, sweating and even fainting. In her books she really only has two types of female, those like herself, and those like Ella and Norah, who were given masculine reactions, and deep voices. Mary Bastard came into the first category, Violet Ebsworth into the second. For male copy she had Reggie, weak and self-indulgent, Tom the chauffeur, quiet, unassuming and reliable, and Gerald and his brothers, confident, brave and single-minded. Of the artistic or musical mortal she knew one one, except A. S. Watt, who could count as a friend, and who was in fact the only man she knew at all well outside her immediate family circle. His erudition and long experience of how to handle writers must have made him a very charming person for her to meet, quite unlike anyone else Ethel ever met. She never expanded her circle, except to give a dinner party once a year to next-door neighbours who did not greatly interest her, but who were on her conscience until she had dutifully wined and dined them. Never one to go out and meet people, she retreated yet further into herself after her operation.

In some of her books, Ethel seems preoccupied with writing about delirium, and the delusions caused by high fever. Scarlet fever, which all the Dell children had experienced in their early teens, would have given Ethel an insight into the fevered mind. Although too late to be called Victorian, her childhood was full of the proximity of sudden death, if not in her own home then in the houses of friends and relations. Brain fever is several times mentioned; with no antibiotics until well after the Great War, meningitis in those days was a sure killer. There was nothing unusual then about being haunted by the fear of illness and death, whereas now, though there may be just as much suffering, trust in modern drugs seems to have ousted the instinct to pray to God for deliverance. Drugs have not superseded God, but outshone Him. God is not turned to except in extremes, whereas formerly his aid was being constantly sought. This makes some of Ethel's writing hard going—to cry openly for help is no longer 'done'. We are more independent, less gentle and trusting. Ethel constantly put her hand in the hand of God, and allowed herself to be led along the path of righteousness. Had her father not married a Protestant and dropped his Catholic faith, she might well have gone into a convent like her aunt, Mother Mary Alphonsine who had been Superior of the Redemptoristine Convent in Chudleigh since 1925, or her cousin, now Dame Joan McLaughlin who went into the enclosed convent of Stanborok Abbey, when she was twenty-four, who after ten years there found herself in charge of their famous printing press which now produces beautiful limited editions. Today she is a very old lady, but she has a much happier expression on her face than either of her Dell cousins ever did. Ella's attitude towards these good women was sneering and intolerant, Ethel's far more gentle and appreciative. One wonders whether it may not have been to her Aunt Mary that she went for advice, and to receive Godly help and blessing that summer before her engagement to Gerald. If she did go, Ella would certainly not have been told.

Ethel was getting older, fifty-two on 2nd August, 1933; it showed in her writing and she seemed older than Ella who was fifty-four. She was also lingering longer over descriptions of places, passions were less impulsive, life was beginning to run more slowly and thoughtfully. Her fire had not been quenched, but it was better controlled, so burned with more telling effect when the breath of passion seared. She had always planned her books with care but now that her craftsmanship was more polished she wrote better, if less dramatically. Accordingly her sales began to tail off. Gently; nothing remarkable, but her books went into fewer editions.

During this period both sisters tried to accept life as it came rather than to reach for an ideal existence. Ella openly showed affection for her sister, and physically attempted to be pleasant to Gerald, not entirely for her own sake but partly for Ethel's. If Ella rang Ethel up, the possibility that Gerald might answer was so disturbing that Ella would walk up and down the dining room, glancing at the telephone on top of the Adam chest, patting her mouth in silent prayer before asking for the number. So determined was she to sound pleasant that she would sometimes discuss with me some hobby or other of Gerald's so that it should be fresh in her mind, and she could sound interested. It was advisable for me to be there to make encouraging faces until Ethel came on the line, when I would slink away to let them talk peacefully.

To harbour such a dislike to anyone is a great burden; Ella was never free of it, jealousy ate into her soul like a chafing pack-strap. Ethel knew this and wrote in *The Electric Torch* a year or so later, 'But jealousy isn't love, my dear, even I know that, it's a very poor imitation. Heaven deliver me from jealousy, it's rank poison, nothing else.' That Ethel understood how Ella felt must have communicated itself to Ella.

The relationship between the two sisters is brought to mind in Ethel's *The Electric Torch*. Ella loved Ethel with hedonistic possessiveness and Claire in this novel strongly reminds me of the way in which Ella used to describe Ethel as a young girl.

Claire, slight, pale, almost insignificant in the opinion of the majority. And yet it was Claire who took the lead, and

Claire upon whom the elder girl leaned. . . . Claire was a
person of strange ideals, though intensely reticent by nature,
she made no secret of her devotion to her sister, practically
all the women in the station disapproved of [Yvonne], but
Claire remained her staunch supporter. . . . She [Claire] went
with him submissively, her slim white figure drooping, her
pale face thoughtful, Yvonne had told her she ought to wear
white, she was too colourless for it, yet there was something
in Claire's white attire that had its own appeal. Her pallor
was too fine to suffer by contrast.

Correspondingly, it was upon Ethel that her elder sister
leaned. Although there was much of the champion in Ella's
attitude, in fact it was Ethel who set the tone, and of this Ella
was afraid. She did not want to hurt Ethel but had a still more com-
pelling reason to curb her instincts; to be Ethel's sister was not
merely prestigious, it was materially very rewarding.

Sweet aloof Ethel, who never raised her voice in anger, and
one is tempted to believe never thought evil about anyone, continued to enchant and awe all who came in contact with her.
Domestics who worked for her, even if only for a short period,
felt that her dark blue eyes could see into their souls and were
consequently inhibited from telling lies, or stealing, thus bene-
fiting from her good and gentle influence. Not that Ethel ever
said much, her quiet presence was apparently enough to inspire
great loyalty.

My own position put me into the unfortunate role of observer
and judge of both sisters. Ethel disliked me, and I am probably
the only person about whom she allowed herself to feel in this
way; indeed a backhanded honour. Ella loved me, but again
jealousy was to ruin even that relationship.

What I suspect Ethel would have liked me to be is contained
in the only wholly sad book she ever wrote. *Dona Celestis* is the
study of an orphan, a beautiful, talented girl, who is taken
advantage of by one man, married out of pity by another, loses
her only child, and is publicly disowned by her rightful mother.
That none of these things was likely to happen to me, made the
writing of the book a necessity, a warning and also a lesson in
gratitude.

Ella never allowed the book into the house, and I first read it

only recently. Ethel liked her women to be conspicuously help-
less and feminine; fortunately Ella had seen to it that I had
plenty of worldly experience and was unlikely to suffer the fate
of 'Dona Celestis'. Ethel's warning did not reach me, and even
if it had I doubt if the message would have penetrated. I would
certainly have wept, but not for myself. Nothing was more
appealing to Ethel than purity, trust, innocence, and naiveté;
I had none of these in any measurable degree.

Dona Celestis, published in 1933, was one of the most ambitious studies in human relationships that Ethel ever attempted.
It certainly ranks as her most brilliant piece of human observation. It succeeds in that she was not pleasing anyone but
herself. The writing benefits enormously from this; there are
no sops to the sentimental reader, the story is told directly and
graphically and there are some tragic passages which show no
sign of overwriting. Ethel could do it if she wished, but unfortunately her unselfishness often swayed her better judgment,
and she could not bear to disappoint her public. In *Dona Celestis*
there is little or no pandering to public taste.

Unfortunately, when Ethel wrote about what really interested
her, her regular readers did not appreciate it, and others had
already been put off her work by reading adverse reviews. Her
name was synonymous with 'trash'; no one who valued his
intellectual reputation would have been seen dead reading one
of her novels. The slowing-down in her readership now became
a slacking off. Very few copies of *Dona Celestis* were sold, her
magic was on the wane. A. S. Watt evidently took a hand in her
future productions and advised her to return to her Indian
romances. This was what the public wanted, so with com-
mendable obedience her next novel was set in that continent,
amongst Indian army officers and their wives and sweethearts.
Except for a few rather glaring slips in topography and nomen-
clature, it emerges as a very successful novel, a return to her
normal image.

A. P. Watt and her public must have breathed a sigh of
relief, particularly A. S. Watt, to whom the book is dedicated.

Some indication of the hurt that Ethel felt at the comparative
rejection of her later and better-written books, comes out in
the following passage from *The Electric Torch*. It is her appeal
to be reassessed; she did not enjoy her reputation for turning out

passionate nonsense, and longed to be taken seriously for the last few years of her working life.

'That's where I might be useful,' he pointed out. 'The strong silent husband—keeping all impertinent enquirers at bay! I believe I could be quite good at that—if you would give me the chance.'

'Don't,' she said.

He smiled at her openly. 'It's what the critics would call a typical "Ethel M. Dell situation". By the way that woman has my sympathy if any woman ever had. She is branded for life on account of her juvenile efforts of umpteen years ago.'

'I don't like her,' said Claire. 'She portrays a world that is hopelessly out of date.'

His smile broadened. 'But the pendulum swings back. And after all, human nature doesn't vary in the long run. Only customs—like eyebrows and things. She isn't what you would call the sophisticated type. But—can anyone say that sophistication will last?'

'I don't know,' said Claire. 'It's nice of you to sympathise with her anyway.'

'I always sympathise with the downtrodden,' he said. 'Don't you?'

'I don't know,' she said again. 'I think my outlook on things is fairly fluid. But I don't like being rushed into things.'

'Like marriage?' he suggested.

'With an Ethel M. Dell hero,' she added smiling for the first time.

'I'm neither ugly enough nor handsome enough for that,' he protested. 'Merely drab and ordinary—but quite ready for use.'

As a story *The Electric Torch* has weaknesses—predictable in the sick woman, hard shudders, and the belief that pale, drooping women are sexually attractive. Predictable in its enchanting sloppy dog, and alas, when it comes to retribution, riding crops are again put to vigorous use, and there is even a vicious kicking. But new and refreshing is a cockney batman, easily the most attractive character—although secondary to the story. Ethel has excelled herself with cockney humour and sagacity,

Peters and the bull terrier bitch remain in one's mind long after the book is finished, both are delightful. Here Tom the chauffeur must be credited with many of the witticisms, though it is hard to realise that only forty years ago such benevolent autocracy was practised by the employer that a batman was expected to receive his master's consent before marriage.

A characteristic description in the book is of a woman in tongue-tied distress: 'She beat her hands soundlessly together with a movement almost the more violent for its repression.'

When writing about India, Ethel never understood that in great tropical heat one does not linger over handshakes or other more private skin contact; sweat is sticky. Perhaps her own experience had not gone beyond a moist upper lip, a slightly downy one which trembled with suppressed mirth, very unnerving if one did not know what she was finding so funny.

Her characters' ears were another trouble to her and she could never attune them to the ridiculous, once set on the path of passion. 'The song of the nightingale thrilled like a clarinet through the odorous stillness.' It was Ella who was musical, and naturally she had not been consulted.

Rest Harrow, like any other house Ella lived in, rang to the sound of her piano, and her voice was still remarkably resonant. A new friend, an elegant young man, one of the sons of the houseboat family in Dorset, was now a firm admirer, they played Brahms' duets, and Ella sang for him. Chopin's two Opus 15 nocturnes were in constant demand. Maurice Bowra had glittered away and been superseded. The rock garden was a mass of colour. Beside the drawing room she had surrounded her rose-trees with blue gentians, and edged them with Mrs. Sinkins's white 'pinks'. The hot colour was dazzling, she was actively happy and slightly coy with her new young friend. Like Ethel she was always generous, and liked to be able to spoil the young.

NINETEEN

The Hut

ALTHOUGH SHE published nothing in 1935, Ethel was working steadily—still riding her tosh horse, but without enthusiasm.

Where Three Roads Meet was published in America the following year; clearly it had been re-written from a manuscript started during the 1914–18 war. She evidently found it difficult to put herself back twenty years and pick up the atmosphere again.

It is strange that she allowed a book with such an obvious plot and laborious dialogue to be published. There was no need for money, and the story does not fit in with any other of her books, its characters are stiff and unbelievable. It has a flavour of *The Princesses' Game*, the abrupt, unpolished sentences seem to have been constructed in the same frame of mind. Is it possible that she could have allowed someone to ghost-write a book for her? It seems an unworthy thought, were it not for the pressures of her public who demanded at least a book a year from her. If this were so, her excuse was not gain, but peace of mind. If her readers were really so uncritical, it might have been tempting to pay someone to hash up an old rejected idea. It is to her credit that she could better the result if she wished.

St. Mary's was still their home, but a plot of land at Weeke was occupying a good deal of Gerald's and Ethel's attention. Their requirements for a new house had been sent out to several architects, and the various designs were excitedly discussed. With money no object, their quest was for artistic effect married to convenience.

The summer of 1936 was hot and beautiful. I had left school at seventeen the year before, and on that birthday had been given an Austin Seven, so by the summer of the following year, when it was time to shut up Rest Harrow and take ourselves down to the Hut in Dorset, I had been driving about seven months. One of Reggie's sons usually spent his summer with us, so it was arranged that I should start off with him and a little luggage, to be followed by Ella driving her own car filled with the rest of the food and cases, and my dog Rags. Jessica the collie was put into the kennels, being too nervous to travel. R. and I drove the hundred and thirty miles without mishap—my first long drive. We immediately started unpacking and to set in order the Hut which had not been used for a year. There were sheets to be aired on gorse bushes, mattresses to drag into the sun, and a mouse-nest in one of the cupboards to be dealt with. A great sweeping, opening of windows and cleaning of floors. R. and I decided to have it all spick and span to welcome Ella who was due to arrive about two o'clock.

R. ran off to tell the nearby farm that we had arrived and to get Bert the cowhand to bring us some drinking water from a spring just below the Hut site. It was a very hot day, we were both in Hut clothes. R. just in shorts and myself in shirt and shorts. By four o'clock Ella had not arrived and I began to be anxious, trying desperately not to show it too much; R. had enough family troubles without any added ones on holiday with us. By six o'clock, I was wondering if I ought to drive to the nearest telephone some eight miles away to inform the police, when I saw what appeared to be a rhinoceros charge in slow motion advancing towards the Hut over the dusty dirt track, plumes of feathery dust curling up behind. As it drew near, the centre of the dark swaying dipping motion glinted and proved to be a very large grey saloon car heaving towards us. At the same time Bert arrived with his two pails of spring water slung on a yoke; his face lengthened into open-mouthed wonder.

The huge limousine stopped beside the Hut, a chauffeur got out and opened the door to—of all people—Uncle Gerald. Seeing me coming to greet him, he called out, 'My God, what a hole—is this what you call having a nice holiday?' Then with great care he picked his way between the gorse bushes (still draped with sheets) and, brushing his military moustache in disapproval of the scene—which included Bert, who by now had put the buckets down and was picking little bits of dried bracken off the surface of the water with his dirty fingers—announced, 'Your aunt has had an accident; ran into the back of another car and cracked her ribs'. 'Will she be all right?' was all I could think of saying. He looked at me, and snorted, 'Of course she will, take a lot more than that to put paid to your Aunt Ella'.

Foolishly, but meaning well, I asked him to stay and have supper, as he had come such a long way; looking about him, he took in the camping accoutrements which were in evidence. Mentally pulling up the hem of his trousers, he turned towards me; 'Very kind, but the tin plates are a little too reminiscent of the war, and I still have to negotiate my return, Packards are not built for dirt roads, and Tom didn't enjoy the drive'. I looked at Tom sitting in the car. Did I imagine it or did he wink as he touched his cap? Gerald continued, 'Your aunt will stay with us for a few days, her car is a write-off, so I suppose she will get another one to drive over in, oh yes, she sent her love, and said you were not to worry'. He looked around again and added, 'Just carry on as usual'.

As he was getting back into his newest toy, I remembered my dog, beloved Rags and asked if he was safe. 'That dog? Oh yes, your aunt's a bit upset, he's lost, but I daresay your Aunt Ethel will drive over to the place where it happened, and see if she can call him, you know her talents!'

I must have looked upset, as he pulled down the window as he was leaving and called out. 'You'll be all right will you, in this Godforsaken place?' I assured him we would, grateful for his rough concern, but glad to see him go.

Ella stayed with Gerald and Ella for about two weeks, eventually arriving in a brand new car, looking chastened and pale. Rags was never found, although Ethel had driven over and called and called, he was either dead or did not respond to a comparative stranger's voice. Months later Tom told me that she had walked up and down the road, calling until her voice went, tears streaming down her cheeks, and this for a dog she hardly knew. Dear Ethel, her emotions were so easily touched.

Ella had not been back at the Hut more than a day or so when yet again we were called upon, but now by the Law. A hot and dusty policeman arrived on a bike, with a summons for Ella to attend the magistrates' court in Alton. The Bobby was delighted to accept tea, and went off, unlike Gerald, with apologies for having brought bad news.

We all three drove over for the court hearing. Ella was fined and her licence suspended for three months, so I had to drive us all back in her new car. That summer I became officially adult and Ella could at last admit that it was pleasant to accept (very occasionally) a sharing of responsibility. At fifty-seven she walked, talked and argued like a woman ten years younger. Only her clothes gave her away, they were still smart, but now too conventional to be interesting.

Much of Ethel's novel *Where Three Roads Meet* is devoted to sympathy with a young wife who is not in love with her husband, and is thankful that although his love was 'like a devouring monster, always craving, never satisfied', it did not, she thought pathetically, ask for more than 'the outer husk'; she considers herself fortunate, as this was all she had to give. Something there is familiar, it is said with sympathy as if she knew so well how the girl felt, yet again one wonders just how much she herself enjoyed physical love. Where she is really at home, is in the lead-up to a passion which is not consummated, leaving one, or both, paranoiacally frustrated. Perhaps this answers the question which is being begged throughout her writing. She preferred to defer, but would succumb out of charity. Her nature was sentimental rather than warm.

Seeing Gerald stamping disapprovingly about in front of the Hut gave me an adult warning, my first frisson of fright. Here was a frustrated man, not a happy husband; women's intuitions are seldom quite wrong, even those of very young women.

Gerald's mother had died in 1935, leaving Norah, now on her own, free to counsel him when she felt so inclined. Her advice generally took the form of telling him exactly how to run his life and influence Ethel to his advantage. In *Where Three Roads Meet*, Caroline, the dominant elder sister of Lord Aubreystones, derives much of her speech and manners from Norah, who was apt to trample on people's ideals with a certain amount of ruthless pleasure. Norah was a capable woman there is no doubt, even worthy and talented. She could produce passable watercolours, and was said to have a good head for money.

Reggie, now living in Brighton, calling his house Wykeham Lodge, the only one of the family to use their ancestor's name, had by now produced three sons. One had died, one was in a home, and R, their last hope, was in his teens, and determined at that time to enter the navy. When he came on holiday with us he was on leave from a naval establishment at Havant. Reggie's youngest child, a daughter, Patricia, was in a special school near Crowborough, chosen and paid for by Ella. It was close enough for us to keep an eye on her and take her out over weekends, but unlike R. she did not accompany us to the Hut.

Reggie continued to make his number with Ella, bringing his sick wife over with him. These were horrifying visits, but Ella was determined to keep Reggie so much in her debt that he would allow her control over his children, thus ensuring they were looked after properly. Ethel did not meet Reggie's wife, I suspect because she knew Gerald's attitude to slovenliness and what he would regard as disintegration.

What a passionate moralist Ethel is. In every book a lesson is wrapped up in its sentimental pages. The moral in *Where Three Roads Meet* seems to be that spiritual love can overcome any obstacle—even a 'dead' lover returning with a transformed face, a miracle of plastic surgery given to him to cover his identity as a disfigured deserter from the War, and re-establish him as a man. How she enjoys making this man into a masochist, bewailing his past sins, and enjoying every minute of it, to the distress of his erstwhile mistress (called politely his wife), who had recognised him by the light in his eyes and by his stance.

There is something macabre about the idea of a nerveless pale mask of skin being passionately kissed, not so much for physical reasons as for the idea of a totally new face years younger than the body and unlikely to age, the muscles being unable to contract the skin sufficiently to create kindly wrinkles. Spiritual love, we are led to suppose, leads the way back to physical passion, re-kindled after twenty years of separation. The intervening years had involved the heroine in a coldly aristocratic marriage and having six children, the first of these and then a seventh being attributable to the transformed lover.

Why do all Ethel's later heroines have to be tired, ill, exhausted, and ready to faint when the going stiffens up? It was not fashionable; the thirties were hard and fast. One wonders why Ethel's idea of the total woman, the essence of femininity, had to be so frail, why she imagined that a man could be more easily wound round a woman's little finger if she was as fragile as a flower? None of her more masculine types get married, nor did they in her worldly experience. Ella, Norah,

Violet Ebsworth, all these able women never made marital
vows. So if Ethel herself had been feminine one could understand
her attitude. But she was not. Getting on now, her grey hair
was winged with white over each ear, while her tweed suits and
brogues, her deep husky voice, and lack of all makeup, pro-
claimed her sexual ambiguity.

That she liked the utterly feminine type, may reveal a leaning
towards lesbianism of which she was unaware. Ethel would
never have contemplated anything so abhorrent. Ella conversely,
wept openly when she learnt of Virginia Woolf's death by
drowning—not so much for the method, but for the loss, referring to Vita Sackville West as 'That awful woman'. A jealous
reaction no doubt, and a natural dislike of another masculine
type.

In the summer when most women, even the most masculine,
put on light clothes, Ethel still wore her dull skirts and blouses;
certainly of thinner material, but in drab colours. She had not
changed over all the years, and it is even recorded in her own
hand, her dislike of progress, and preference for things past.

> Looking back to the old dear pre-War world, she realised
> how different life had been. There had been time in those days
> to breathe, to live, to be happy. People had not developed the
> fighting instinct. Games had been games, not fierce contests
> for supremacy. And work had been a peaceful thing that
> brought its own reward, not a mad competition for the highest
> gain, the shortest hours, and the greatest amount of leisure.
> It seemed to her that life had become a rather feverish litter of
> unwanted things. No one stopped to think. They merely
> threw aside what seemed superfluous and tore on. Whither?
> Ah, whither indeed! The litter was so pathetic too, sometimes
> really good stuff that might have been turned to fair account,
> sometimes piteous broken objects to which the owner alone
> could have given a name, sometimes actual treasure discarded
> in sheer caprice. (*Where Three Roads Meet*)

Ethel was not the only person of her class to miss the first
indications that there was another world conflagration about to
ignite, what she was seeing were the first signs that all was not
well below the surface. Ethel was still very much an Edwardian
at heart.

Rollo, the first child of Molly, heroine of *Where Three Roads Meet*, may well be Ethel's idea of a son. Her description of the two together, although almost sexually aberrant and irritatingly soppy, does pull the heartstrings. She would obviously have adored to have had such a boy, possibly without too much human intervention.

It makes one wonder if she suffered from delusions of Marydom, not so uncommon amongst gifted and imaginative women, with Rollo's father wearing a transfigured face, and repeatedly asserting that he is not worthy.

Ethel even confesses her minor sins, admitting that she knows quite well that 'reticence with the press attracts curiosity' and that 'try to evade attention, and people are after you like a pack of hounds'. So she did enjoy being mysterious and hard to get at after all!

With the house at Weeke now almost complete, 1937 was a year of great upheaval. Gerald was constantly on the site; if he could have re-aligned every brick he would have done so. It drove the builders into gloom, and the architect into a frenzy, forever having to make last-minute adjustments and additions. For Gerald, however, this was his great achievement, he was in his natural element. His army training served him well, emphasising his passion for detail and encouraging him to check every quantity and survey procedure.

In March he took time off to go down to the biggest of the Winchester bookshops where Ethel's latest novel, *Honey Ball Farm* was on display. They had taken up a whole window advertising her as an example of local talent, with reviews and blow-ups of the dust cover to attract attention. He paused outside, asked a stranger what it was all about, and was smartly put in his place for not having heard of Ethel M. Dell, which delighted him. He then made the mistake of going inside, hoping to repeat the performance, but the bookseller recognised him at once, and gave the show away, to his disgust. He retold this story to Ethel over lunch, and she remonstrated gently with him; 'Gerald darling, you shouldn't have gone inside.' Their parlourmaid recounted it all to the cook who decided that 'The colonel was stupid to think no one knew him' and then added, 'just the sort of silly thing he would do'.

Ethel herself had that very morning been doing up presents of this novel to be sent to close relatives and friends. Ella received hers with the following letter inside.

> St. Mary's,
> Winchester,
> 1 March, 1937

My own darling Elizabeth,

Here is my new book with my very best love. It came out last Thursday. I do hope that you will like it darling.

How are you? Not snowed up, I hope!

Have you heard any more about Uncle Will? I mustn't stay for more now, as I have several other parcels to send off.

My very best love, darling,

> Always your own most loving
> Nettie.

The immediacy of this letter is interesting; she treats it as if she were face to face with her sister. The reference to Uncle Will was a hint to Ella, as eldest in the family, that it was for her to know and pass on information about their Uncle. In fact he was ill and died not long afterwards. He was the last of his generation which left Ella, in years, head of the family. Ella missed Uncle Will more than Ethel did; he had been one of the very few men in her life of whom she had been genuinely fond and his going was unexpectedly sudden. I had never seen her so saddened before, and it confirmed my belief that she was softer than she pretended. During several evenings following his funeral she told me about their childhood love for Uncle Will and Aunt May, showing me photographs of him as a young and dapper bachelor, and, after much hunting, a small black notebook which contained instructions for various parlour games in his neat hand, and joy of joys, a series of 'pigs' drawn with the eyes shut, and each signed. They are an interesting revelation of divergent characters, the angular effort of Ella's pig contrasting neatly with Ethel's gently dreamy one.

Honey Ball Farm was partly true, or as the synopsis says on the fly leaf 'it was not the outcome of pure imagination'. Who were these people? One hesitates to believe that there could have been real-life models for a story so macabre and horrifying. Ethel gives her imagination full reign, happily describing the flogging of a girl of nineteen by her revoltingly sadistic father.

There are dried mummy heads to be seen by torchlight, a bedroom fit for a dirty prisoner, not an innocent young woman, curtains which drop to pieces and cobwebs over fixed windows. The background is darkness, slimy moisture, and unexplained slithering noises.

Excitement and intrigue are sustained from the first page to the last. In spite of agonising experiences which include being corded up in a sack and thrown on her father's bed to await his vengeance, this innocent girl has Grit. Though subjected to vile gossip, and to days at sea with a viking 'god' of a man, which leave her intrigued but strong enough to resist temptation, this 'beautiful peach of a girl' reaches the altar an unsullied virgin. There is a perceptive and sensitive description of the girl's feelings on receiving her first kiss, and some of the dialogue, particularly where it involves the more sophisticated secondary hero and heroine, is excellent though Ethel is still capable of such inadvertent slips as writing 'viscous' when she clearly meant 'vicious'.

The hypocrisy of the well-heeled youth of the 30s is nicely underlined. On the possibility of a lost virginity, 'She can't have gone wrong yet', in the tone of one debating curdled milk. Catty, too; 'None so chaste as them who never had the chance to be anything else.' Relying too much on lost memories and fainting fits, Ethel brings round her patients with milk and rum, tea, or cold milk, and the sight of a loved one brings one girl out of a seemingly fatal trance.

The indispensable 'class' prop in all her later work is the cigarette, acting as a cover for embarrassment, a prop in un-uncertainty, a relief in fright, and a toy to play with between the mouths of lovers. Smoke was blown into faces, kisses exchanged between puffs. Anger could be emphasised by the half-smoked butt ground under heel, frustration by deep inhalation.

Ethel wrote well about boats. She was fascinated by the sea and all that was either rocked on it, or pounded by its strength. Her ear for sea noises was perfectly tuned and her interiors of small cabin cruisers in a choppy sea are realistic enough to induce seasick reading, though the weather has an irritating tendency to change miraculously from storm to sunshine to suit each turn of the plot.

Massive masculine shoulders and powerful arms evidently

had great appeal, as did huge dark eyes, abundant hair, and a peach-coloured skin. Her male lead is dominant and magnetic, her two heroines attractively contrasted with each other. One may however experience a sense of unease on reading that the only tunes that the hero can whistle are 'Cavalleria Rusticana' and 'Abide with Me', both performed with 'exquisite cadences'.

Honey Ball Farm was a success. Ethel's body may have been ailing, but her mind was alert; she still knew how to 'hook' her public.

TWENTY

Final Move

THE HOUSEHOLD which moved from St. Mary's to Meadow-lands consisted of Ethel, Gerald, Tom Blomfield and his wife, Jean the cook, and Frances the parlourmaid. Tom's duties were as chauffeur to them both and companion-batman to Gerald. Mrs. Tom was not strong, and had no duties except as a wife and mother to their daughter Hilda. The Blomfields moved into a small house acquired for them just up the road from the new house; it had no running water or bath, and the lavatory was in the garden.

This did not worry their employers, even when Tom fell into a pond trying to fish out one of Gerald's toy motor boats. He was not allowed to take a bath in the servant's bathroom at Meadowlands, but had to tote buckets of hot water from the kitchen, while still wearing his freezing wet clothes. He had brought back Gerald who had also taken a ducking, and while the water was heating in the buckets on the stove, Gerald could be heard singing in his own hot bath upstairs. This was not deliberate cruelty, it was accepted behaviour to someone you employed as a servant. At Ella's it was the same; she and I had baths every day but Mr. and Mrs. Gilbert were allowed a bath only once a week. Ella used to wrinkle her nose behind Mrs. Gilbert's back by Friday, which was not surprising, and nearly always made a point of going out somewhere on bath day, taking me with her, and then rather ostentatiously opening all the upstairs windows on her return. Horribly offensive, but even as recently as 1937 servants were not supposed to have feelings. Had Ethel's attention been drawn to the fact that Tom was still in his wet uniform long after Gerald had changed into fresh clothes and was downstairs warming himself by the fire, she would I am sure, have been very distressed, but in those days servants did not complain.

The day before moving the furniture into Meadowlands, Gerald went over in the evening to make a final check, and see that all was ready for 'boarders'. The parquet flooring had just been finished and he wanted to gloat over its beauty before it was covered in rugs and furniture.

To his horror, almost in the middle of the drawing room floor, a huge scarlet stain spread its gory fingers over an area three or four feet square. It was six o'clock and the specialist workmen had gone, but without hesitation Gerald telephoned to the firm's manager and made it clear that unless the stain was removed by eight o'clock next morning, he would sue him.

The workmen responsible were collected from their homes, the offending floor was pulled up, replaced and repolished to match the rest of the parquet. Just as the furniture van arrived, six exhausted employees trailed out of the house, the job completed. It had taken them all night, and the cause? A large tin of pink Ronuk polish, upended by the polishers who had been working all over the house.

Gerald was extremely efficient. It could sometimes be irritating to the kitchen staff who disliked interference. One of his annual jobs as a reserve officer was to check stores and the quality of food in barracks. When he returned from one of these exercises, he was apt to wander into the kitchen or scullery, stick a magnifying glass to one eye, and pick up some harmless object such as a loaf of bread or a packet of biscuits, and pretend to see dust and dirt on it. For servants it was far too real to be funny, and their giggles were polite and forced.

If it was a question of changing washers on taps, then he was in his element, doing the job himself efficiently and with pride, but spoiling the effect by taking off and imitating the British workman, to women who came from working class families. To his own family he was a splendid person and much admired.

Spring 1938 saw yet another novel on the market, *The Serpent in The Garden*, the first to be published from her new house. Writing with a certain amount of nostalgia and setting it in the south of France, Ethel recalls the sinister lush atmosphere of sunlight, sea and flower gardens, finding it suitable for her own particular garden of Eden.

Perhaps she had been saving up this particular locality for what she hoped would be her most telling book. What she does achieve is a tale from the heart, irresistibly herself. Part I introduces the actors, her Adam and her Eve, and a devil who is masquerading as an Italian Count, in a tropical Garden of Eden where 'that blaze of flowers is like too much to drink'. The stars, too were 'like jewels on velvet'—a phrase Ethel must have really enjoyed writing; she had used it before, and knew that it pleased her readers. She had no literary pretentions; why should she strain after literary effect? One can see her smiling as she wrote each defiantly successful repetition.

Her Adam is an English Public School boy, the perfect untried man. Her Eve seems innocent and in need of protection, but is in fact cool, provocative, perspicacious and calculating; well able to look after herself, yet simulating naivité. When Eve touches Adam 'her touch was as flint to steel' and she possesses a 'vagrant magnetic smile', so that soon 'he knows the early morning rapture of first love'.

The Italian Count, in truly reptilian fashion, has 'a narrow tense hand, which seems poisonous when grasped'. Ethel is enjoying herself, her steed is oat-fed, and she tramples her critics right and left, under thundering hooves, enjoying the ride as much as her readers . . . it must have been great fun to write, and proved eminently successful. If *Honey Ball Farm* contained Hell, then *The Serpent in the Garden* points the way from Eden to Heaven, with Peter holding the gate open with his big toe, Peter being Ethel's synonym for Adam. Alas, by the end of Part I, Adam has been thrown out of Eden. He is, however, still innocent. The mysterious intrigue which unwinds must be read in the original, no précis could do it justice.

While Ethel was writing this delightful nonsense, Gerald had been setting up his model railway once again, which had not seen the light of day since Ewhurst. It gave him great pleasure to see it running around the estate, he even enticed Ethel on to it once more. But they were both getting on in years, and probably felt a trifle silly, with Tom shovelling chips of coal into the boiler, and the maids standing by to wave them on. Tom was now grizzled, as was Gerald, they were ageing together nicely, and Ethel, older than them both, looked worn and tired, yet was still able to smile happily if relations came to see them in their lovely new house. One of the great advantages to Ethel was its proximity to woods and walks; she could stroll out of her front door, down to the end of their property, and out through a wicket gate into woods with a right of way. There was no risk of meeting the press or amateur photographers hoping to get a glimpse of her and make money with the resulting picture. If fresh air had anything to do with her state of mind, her enthusiastic writing in *The Serpent in The Garden* may have been partly due to her change of environment. Ethel's second book of the same year was published simultaneously in America. It was as if she knew her physical powers were failing, but that she still had something to say, and felt an urgency to get it done before it was too late. *The Juice of the Pomegranite* is a story pounded out with noticeable effort by a determined yet weakened hand.

The *Serpent* had been dedicated to Gerald, for his birthday; but *The Juice of the Pomegranite* was more nostalgic. The dedication runs thus:

> I dedicate this book to the loved memory of one who has passed beyond these earthly shadows, whose precious friendship now shines out to me as a beacon from the land of joyful resurrection. . . . Our partings never parted us, and so though earthly sight could follow you no further, we only said good-night!

Who was the loved one? This remains her secret.

There is one link between this and her last book: the French detective Pierre Ronceau, half brother of her Adam in *The Serpent in The Garden*, comes to the rescue once again.

In *The Juice of the Pomegranite* Ethel allows a bastard to be conceived, revolving the whole plot around this fact. The dreadful deed has been perpetrated by an aristocratic employee of the Chinese Customs, who has a suitably 'chink' visage coupled with a reputation for counter-espionage. The Chinese locality was probably inspired by the Bowra association of many years earlier, yet the heroine's desire to obtain a pilot's licence certainly stems from myself. It was one of my earliest ambitions; the elderly heroine's mother saying, 'don't be wild, my dear' was without doubt Ella—heard admonishing me more in hope than expectation.

Reading the hunting parts conjures up visions of Ethel

mugging up *Horse and Hound*, and then with equal persistence and distaste reading *Vogue* and *The Tatler* for the appropriate fashions and London Society flavour. No one who had factually experienced either milieu would write so diligently about what was supposed to be second nature to the participants.

Yet allow Ethel to take you for a country walk, and her descriptions are so vivid and the picture received so genuine that a vision is permanently planted in the mind; when the same place is mentioned again in the text, there is no trouble picturing the setting.

There are some neat, contracted descriptions too, 'elderly coquetry' says so much more than a long description of mincing smiles, and 'supercilious interest' again neatly shortcuts the need to explain the raised eyebrow in the unbending body. She 'fares forth' several times, a favourite expression with both sisters, whether it were a walk, a trip to London or a picnic. There are some heavily poetic lines too: 'It was one of those golden days that sometimes happen in mid-November when the sweetness of summer seems to return like a wistful spirit to gaze upon the beauty of the dying year'. And when she describes a 'man standing like a defiant stag' on a knoll under the trees, one can only feel relieved that he does not blow steam from his nostrils or bellow his maleness.

Sex is *taken* by the male, and *received* most unwillingly by the female, when the union is not within the bonds of marriage. There is a cracked bell ringing here, for what male would continue to be interested in a passive female, particularly if she has been drugged? It is Ethel excusing her heroine for being human, and then making her incapable of any other action. Again there is emphasis on female illness, fainting, weaknesses, tottering gait and palpitations, with dressing gowns, hot-water-bottles and hot doctored milk to the rescue.

Everything comes right in the end, of course; the wicked husband is killed in a motor smash, from which the heroine recovers, losing her unwanted child in the process, and marries the man of her heart. Ethel had neither the courage nor the inclination to make it otherwise; her predictability makes this penultimate effort, like all her others, irritating to any readers who are not emotionally deprived. But such were exactly the people for whom Ethel wrote her novels.

Regrettably, she once again touches on her own books in this one. The heroine discovers a book pushed under a cushion and remarks 'Great Scot, it's an Ethel M. Dell! That poor fish. Blanche [owner of the book], I'm beginning to know what's the matter with you. You're a snob, and I'm going to punish you for it. I shall put this book where all your highbrow friends will mark and learn.' Then a page or so further on, the maid says, 'I never leave a Dell book lying about for visitors to see'. 'Ever read them yourself' asked Diana. 'Yes, Madam,' said Enid. 'And you like them?' 'Yes, Madam' Enid said again. Diana lit her cigarette. 'I congratulate you, Enid,' she said. 'We may like bad things, but it isn't all of us who have the courage to say so.' Ethel would have loved Ella to champion her more openly, and this may well be a side-swipe at Ella's intellectual pretensions.

Religiously speaking (and this is what Ethel is doing through-out her work) a most interesting moment comes when on Good Friday a comparative unbeliever goes to pray fervently in a Catholic chapel. The red sanctuary light is glowing, and the priest *deliberately* leaves the chapel door unlocked all night for the sole benefit of the solitary supplicant.

For once Ethel has been tripped up within her own specialised sphere. Good Friday and through to Easter Day are the only days in the year in which the Sanctuary lamp is not alight, signifying the absence of Christ from the Church until Easter morning. Ethel could never have been into a Catholic church on such an occasion, or surely she would have remarked on the hooded statues, the veiled cross and the missing red flame. There would have been no need for the chapel to be especially left open, it would never have been shut over these particular days in the calendar of the Catholic church.

During the summer of 1938 Gerald was complaining of pain in his leg; his balance was unsteady, he was apt to bump into walls, and his speech became very slightly jolting. Ethel was extremly worried, and eventually persuaded him to see a doctor. The diagnosis, disseminated sclerosis mostly affecting his leg.

Yet in the spring of 1939 Gerald's trouble was so slight as to be scarcely noticeable, except to those who knew him well. He sensibly decided to keep it as quiet as possible. He had for years been on the Army's reserve of officers. Now, like most of the world, he suspected that war was imminent, and if only for the sake of his family tradition, he desperately wanted to be called up and take a useful part again.

Ethel knew it was a long-drawn-out, irreversible disease, which would painfully progress into total disability. She was shocked and saddened. Far from well herself, she too began to fail in health, becoming extremely thin and breathless. Ella rang up one evening, unaware of Gerald's condition. He answered the telephone, and hearing his jerky speech, she jumped to the conclusion that he had been drinking. She joked with him for a few minutes until Ethel arrived to take the receiver. Then in her usual direct way Ella proceeded to inform Ethel that she knew exactly what was wrong with Gerald. 'You've been celebrating, haven't you, Gerald sounded as if he'd had quite enough.' Her laugh had a melodic and superior ring to it. Ethel merely said 'Oh, Sissie, how could you be so cruel?' and hung up. The last time she had said this had been when she had announced her engagement to Gerald, and Ella had suggested he was only after her money. Twice in a lifetime was evidently too much.

Ella came back into the drawing room where we had been sitting; she looked very upset and told me what had happened. We discussed the possibilities, and decided that in all probability Gerald did have a liking for the bottle, and that Ethel had been shielding him. With Ella's experience of Reggie's wife, she could be excused the mistake as no alternative explanation had been offered.

To make things worse, Ella then wrote Ethel a most sympathetic letter, apologising for having stumbled on the truth. Ethel took this as just one more burden to be borne, and far from enlightening Ella of her tragic mistake, kept silence, neither answering Ella's letter or coming to the telephone. If Ella rang up, Gerald answered and told her that Ethel was busy writing. In all her life Ella had never been excluded from Ethel's confidence, she felt frustrated and furious with Gerald, who unbeknownst to her was innocent of anything more than a mortal disease.

Although ill and exhausted Ethel continued to write, starting her final novel in the early summer. Their lovely new house which should have been a great joy to them, had been completed too late for them to see it in its maturity, the garden was still a field, the sweep in front of the house had been planted with young trees. Ella had given them masses of daffodils to naturalise, helping to plant them herself. These bloomed for the first time that fateful spring of 1939. There was talk of getting in a landscape gardener, but not much was done about it, the news was bad, and then Gerald got his call-up notice; he was needed in Hertford.

With the efficiency of a major campaigner, he let Meadowlands and repaired to Hertford, taking Ethel with him—for once she was given little choice. Tom accompanied them and they stayed in the same hotel which had sheltered them during their first year of marriage. Apart from sending her change of address, Ethel did not write to Ella; there was a total freeze between them, a wretched misunderstanding which neither side could fathom.

Ethel soon became not only thin and breathless, but unable to sleep, in constant pain, and finding her new book *Sown amongst Thorns* almost impossible to write. Without telling Gerald she went to London and visited the Harley Street man who had performed her mastectomy. He diagnosed general cancer, and as no one ever told lies to Ethel, informed her that she might have another five or six months to live, and gave her pain-killing pills.

Romantic and sentimental Ethel may have been, but with regard to her personal health she was practical and courageous. She told Gerald at once, not believing in beating about the bush. It was now obvious that she would go first, so with admirable courage she saw her solicitor and made a final will on the seventh day of July 1939, leaving everything to Gerald to do as he liked with. He would be needing all the support he could get with a future as a permanent invalid.

Ethel's next call was to the undertakers. She needed, she said, to be buried as far as possible from anyone else, and was prepared to pay for the plot now. Hertford Cemetery is large, there are still areas which have yet to be used. Ethel chose a place well away from any other graves, in a pleasant, peaceful situation, where her beloved birds could sing in the trees over her head. I am sure it comforted her to think that she should end her days in the town where she had first shared life with Gerald.

Then she returned to the hotel to try and complete her book and await death.

Gerald was not then in much pain but he had trouble in keeping his dragging leg from showing, excusing it as rheumatism and hoped to hang on and be useful. If there was to be what he called 'a bust up', he wanted to be there.

Ella knew little of this. Norah had written to her saying that neither of them were well, but not giving details. The summer dragged on into early autumn, Ethel finished her book, and went into a private nursing home. Norah came over and stayed with Gerald, who by now could see for himself that Ethel did not have much longer in this world and was devastated with grief. When Ella, suspicious of so much silent conspiracy, rang up, Norah told her that Ethel was indeed ill in hospital, but did not want to see her. Ella found this hard to believe. Her darling Nettie had always wanted her near when she was ill. Ella was being pushed out and she knew it, sorrowing in silence.

I was at home, also waiting to be called up, having done two years training as a F.A.N.Y. A sense of impending catastrophy hung over us all.

On the 3rd September war was declared. I was called up immediately and went off to Newhaven. Ella rang the hospital hoping to have a word of comfort with Ethel, but she was again coolly told that Mrs. Savage was still no better, and did not wish to see anyone except her husband. A week later Norah rang up again, and told Ella that Ethel was dying, but still did not wish to see her.

To Ella this seemed like gross interference, she did not believe Norah, and promptly drove off in her car to Hertford determined to gain admittance at all costs. I was not at home, but when she rang me up to say she was off to see Ethel, I was pleased, knowing how bruised her feelings had been.

When Ella arrived at the nursing home she decided that her only chance was to charge up to the room and play it by ear from there. This she did, only to find Norah on duty outside like a jailor, evidently expecting Ella's appearance. Ella pushed past her, and tried the handle of the door—it was locked. Norah had by then crossed to the other side of the corridor and was watching the scene. Ella knocked, calling out 'Nettie darling, Nettie, it's me, Sissie, let me in'. A hatch of the door opened and

Gerald's face appeared, weary and white with exhaustion. He shook his head and said, 'She does not want to see you'. Ella gave him one of her most intimidating stares, and informed him that she did not believe him, and rattled the door furiously. A nurse in the corridor laid a restraining hand on Ella's shoulder, and gently asked her to leave, explaining very kindly that it was true that Mrs. Savage did not want to see anyone except her husband.

Ella turned and followed the Sister into her little cubby-hole where she collapsed from sorrow and frustration. Telling me about this years afterwards, Ella could not get to the end of the story without a great outburst of weeping, it had all seemed so cruel and heartless.

On 19th September Ethel died. At the very end, she denied Gerald access as well. But according to hearsay, she died a very brave death, never complaining even in the greatest pain. She was just fifty-eight.

Norah rang Ella and told her briefly, saying that Gerald was so shattered that she was organising all the funeral arrangements, telling Ella where and when it was to take place.

The day before Ethel's funeral, Gerald visited the funeral parlour and knelt beside her coffin weeping almost uncontrollably, then as a farewell gesture, he took from his pocket a large gold cross set with rubies, and placed in in her folded hands, instructing the undertakers to seal up the lid at once.

I came home for the funeral, but at the last minute Ella decided it would be better if I were not there, and refused to let me accompany her.

When she came back she was not, as I expected, in a state of shocked sorrow, but in a much more alarming condition. Arriving home about five o'clock on the day of the funeral, she slammed the car into the garage with a great deal of noise. My sitting room was over it, so I rushed down to greet her with sympathy. She had a light in her eyes that I had never seen there before, so I held back. She passed me with her head held high, scarcely noticed my presence. Flinging down her bag and gloves on the settle in the hall, she strode on to the terrace and began pacing up and down, clenching and unclenching her fists. I had never imagined her in a comparable state, so I was frightened.

After an hour of pacing, she went into the dining room, poured herself out a stiff whisky, and called me in to talk to her. 'We shall have to sell this house, get rid of the dogs, and as long as there's a war and you are needed, I shall move into a smaller house nearer to other people.' She slapped her hand down on tne table, 'And no arguing'. Ella looked fiercely worn out. I did not argue.

The following day Ella sent for the vet, and directed him to destroy Jess the collie, and Sammy, the cairn replacement of the lost Rags. I begged her to change her mind, but she was adamant, and careless of my feelings. 'Go down into the wood, then you won't hear anything,' she commanded. I went, but still couldn't help hearing the sound of two shots. It was horrible. Afterwards Ella returned to normal, it was as if she had ritually slain Norah and Gerald, the air had been cleared, she felt she could breathe properly again.

Ella's ability to recover her composure was astonishing. Any hurt she had suffered, she suppressed, allowing no painful memories to return to the surface until many years later.

Gerald and Norah probably never met or corresponded with Ella again, but some months after Ethel's death Ella received a small box from their Winchester solicitors. It contained what seemed to be a paste bow brooch, and a note to the effect that Col. Savage wished her to have this in memory of her sister. Ella scoffed at what she thought was the final insult. Several years later when having her jewellery valued for insurance, the brooch turned out to be real diamonds. Ella showed it to me with a wry laugh, I turned it over and on the back was the inscription, *From I.E.D. to E.M.D.*, and the date of Ethel's wedding. It had been Ella's own forgotten wedding present to Ethel, the only piece of jewellery she had ever worn other than her wedding and engagement rings. From that moment it became Ella's own favourite brooch. In some way Ethel had been spiritually returned to her. The gap in recognition was a salutory chastening. Ethel herself could not have invented a better way to come back to her.

TWENTY-ONE

Variable Applause

IN HER second book, *The Knave of Diamonds*, written in 1913, Ethel wrote, 'She is one of those women who must run a straight course. There are few such born saints "of whom the world is not worthy".' Was she unwittingly writing her own priggish epitaph? That no one thought of putting it on her gravestone, is sad. Ethel deserved to be remembered by someone from her enormous reading public who could quote her with pleasure.

Even her obituaries were full of snide side-swipes. *The Times*, trying desperately to be fair and detached, placed her with Charles Garvice, Nat Gould, and Edgar Wallace as the most popular novelists in the English-speaking world. Though commenting that her work could be found in the smoking rooms of remote country inns, and that there were no towns and few villages who could not boast a copy of her works, this acknowledgement of success then goes into reverse. 'Their characterization was *perhaps*,* rather thin and stereotyped, and made no appeal to the serious student of literature, but to the ordinary man (and above all woman) in the street, she brought a breath of the wider life with its colour and romance.' There is then a final more generous touch: 'Her books may not come under the heading of literature, but they have given distraction and solace, and entertainment, to many otherwise featureless lives.'

The Times-Literary Supplement confines itself to fact: 'Even though her books could never have appealed to readers of literary discrimination, the name of Ethel M. Dell has its place in the memories of the last War, and the years immediately preceding it and following it.'

The *News Chronicle* ran a full column, with a large heavy type banner heading: *Ethel M. Dell, Best Seller, Dies.* They are more

* My italics. P.D.

164

interested in facts and figures quoting her supposed earnings at
£25,000 a year, and her reading public at nine million, before
getting down to discussing what and how she wrote. Comparing
her with E. M. Hull, they remind us that Ethel's heroes were
strong silent men, and the other ladies' men were sheiks, never
forgetting that her books were 'the quintessence of the novelette
. . . at full length.'

Then there is a typical remark: 'She would smile genuinely but
with a certain inner conviction of her own superiority at the
crudest cracks of the critics.' This is nonsense, she was far too
humble to be superior, but she may well have somewhat smugly
laughed up her sleeve at her own success. This would annoy any
critic. Superiority connotes conceit—a failing with which she
could never have been tagged. Then comes a paragraph headed
'Her Style'. Here they quote verses of Ethel's worst and most
bathetic poetry, guaranteeing her consignment to the realms of
sentimental idiocy. Who would wish to explore the mind of a
woman who could end a verse with 'You are just round the
corner and I am nearing the bend'?

Fortunately for Ethel this *was* her obituary, she was well out
of range, yet what a pity that the next and last remark could not
have reached her; it might have consigned to the realms of
forgetful forgiveness, most of the vicious whippings she had
meekly suffered from the Press. Even meekly enjoyed? 'She was
in private life . . . a woman completely unspoiled by success,
which represented for her a certain satisfaction that her view of
the world—composed of heroes and heroines with no feet of
clay, and villains with no redeeming trait—was the right one,
and, what was more important, the means of gratifying her
lavish generosity. She remained (as a novelist with tens of
thousands of pounds a year), the same devout and industrious
woman she had been when she began (to make her way) rising
at dawn, making her own bed, working when the rest of the
house was asleep, attending church regularly.'

(*News Chronicle*, September 19, 1939)

That she was never praised or compared advantageously to
other novelists during her lifetime must have been somewhat
disappointing, yet her attitude to her work was much the same as
that of Kipling who, according to John Bayley in *The Uses of
Division*, 'does not condescend to intelligence—he is too

absorbed in the ethos of the society he describes'. How sadly obvious it is that to be a successful novelist does not necessarily entail either admiration or approval from that most desirable of quarters, the literary critics.

It must be rare to have written forty novels and a short book of verse without ever squeezing out a grudging 'well written'. There was, however, plenty of contemporary praise for her as an unsurpassed mistress of story telling.

'Miss Dell has the power of vivid writing and good story telling which makes it impossible not to enjoy her story.'
(*Morning Post*)

'Many days and nights must pass before the reader can forget the vivid mental pictures that her writing gives.'
(*Evening Standard*)

'The novel is full of tense situations and highly wrought emotions. Whoever begins it will not put it down until it is finished.'
(*Scotsman*)

'The author of *The Way of an Eagle* has scored another success; indeed it is difficult to express without risk of apparent exaggeration, how good this book is.'
(*Literary World*)

'The story is very vividly written, the characters *nearly* all life like.'
(*Tatler*)

'Full of vivid interest from beginning to end.'
(*Field*)

Four out of these six critics uses the word vivid! But for the people inhabiting her books, they had equal praise, particularly for Nick Ratcliffe, her first hero from *The Way of an Eagle*: 'an original hero who has a heart of gold' (*The Times*); 'a real personality and he lives' (*Evening Standard*); 'a real personality, one of peculiar charm and fascination' (*The Globe*).

Then of Nap Errol, the hero of her second novel, *The Knave of Diamonds*: 'We have no hesitation of claiming for him a place beside many of the most famous and picturesque heroes of the past, not only on account of his furious vitality, but also because of his power to command sympathy even when he is most a rogue' (*Evening Standard*).

No one had any complaints about Ethel's ability to push a pen. Her first publisher, T. Fisher Unwin, made twenty-seven printings—each larger than the last—of *The Way of an Eagle*, between 1912 and 1915. Their indebtedness to her must have been great, as she brought in over half of their already substantial earnings.

Twenty years later, Stevie Smith included Ethel's *The Way of an Eagle* as number eleven in a series run by the *Observer* entitled 'Best Sellers of the Century'. Ethel is admired for respecting human feelings. 'She does try to deal, as Maurice Baring put it, "with the problems of the heart and conscience". Those who eschew feelings have the greatest writers against them as well as Miss Dell.' Stevie Smith's final paragraph must be quoted intact:

> Does this seem absurd to mention Euripides and Shakespeare in an article on the much derided Miss Dell? No, I think not. In its relation to greatness, *The Way of an Eagle* is like Kipling's story of the pseudo Keats, and the light falling not through the stained glass windows of St. Agnes Eve, but through the bright bottles of a chemist's window. Miss Dell's book is not great, but in its small way it is right all the same. Only fools would laugh at Kipling's poor hero. Only fools would laugh at Miss Dell's Nicks and Muriels.

This was written in January 1958, so it is of double interest to read in 1973, a mere fifteen years later, Jilly Cooper in an article (*Sunday Times*, 6th May) entitled 'I pick my team of all time wets', referring to wet writers 'Walt Whitman is a bit of a wet man, and so is D. H. Lawrence, some of his dialogue is pure Ethel M. Dell'. Is being wet synonymous with being a fool? I fear so. Mrs. Cooper has laughed and not for the first time. Ethel would have been honoured at the thought of being bracketed with D. H. Lawrence, Walt Whitman and Wordsworth. But her sense of humour would have delighted in a literary round sung by sundry gentlemen (and ladies) under the personal direction of Marcus Ward (now a learned divine) in the University of Cambridge, *c.* 1927, which went like this:

con brio   Shakespeare, Milton; Shakespeare, Milton;
Shelley as well; Shelley as well,

dim.   Ella Wheeler Wilcox; Ella Wheeler Wilcox,
pp.   Ethel M. Dell; Ethel M. Dell.

Ethel knew her place in the literary hierarchy, she had no pretensions to be other than she was, a Romantic Story Teller.

INDEX

Ethel M. Dell's writings are listed under the entry for Ethel M. Dell herself